THE
STORY
of
ENGLISH

By the same author:

Slippery Tipples: A Guide to Weird & Wonderful Spirits & Liqueurs

Are You Turning Into Your Dad?

THE
STORY
— *of* —
ENGLISH

How an Obscure Dialect
Became the World's
Most-Spoken Language

Joseph Piercy

MICHAEL O'MARA BOOKS

First published in Great Britain in 2012 by
Michael O'Mara Books Limited
9 Lion Yard
Tremadoc Road
London SW4 7NQ

A CIP catalogue record for this book is available from
the British Library.

Papers used by Michael O'Mara Books Limited are natural,
recyclable products made from wood grown in sustainable forests.
The manufacturing processes conform to the environmental
regulations of the country of origin.

ISBN: 978-1-84317-883-5 in hardback print format
ISBN: 978-1-84317-923-8 in EPub format
ISBN: 978-1-84317-924-5 in Mobipocket format

1 3 5 7 9 10 8 6 4 2

Designed and typeset by Design 23

Printed and bound in Great Britain by Clays Ltd, St Ives plc

www.mombooks.com

———✺———

'Language is the
armoury of the human mind,
and at once contains the trophies of its
past and the weapons of its
future conquests.'

SAMUEL TAYLOR COLERIDGE,
ENGLISH POET
(1772–1834)

———✺———

Acknowledgements

I'd like to offer my heartfelt thanks to the following people for their kind help, advice and general fortitude in assisting me with the writing of this book: Mathew Clayton for getting the project off the ground in the first place and his continuing faith and support; Toby Buchan, on account of his limitless patience, intelligence, good humour and kindly encouragement; the design, proofing and picture research teams at Michael O'Mara Books, particularly Jacquie Wines, Ana Bježančević, Ron Callow, Dominique Enright, Greg Stevenson, and Charlotte Buchan (and anybody else who has found my manuscript turn up on their desktop); James Fleet and R. Lucas and all at the University of Sussex Library for letting me use their excellent facilities and fielding my queries, and most of all to Joanna and Polly for allowing me the time and giving me the love and support I require to be in the privileged position to write.

CONTENTS

Introduction

The story of English is one of a struggle for survival against the odds, with centuries of conflict surrounding its development and growth. What with arriving and departing Romans, barbaric Germanic tribes, pillaging Vikings, conquering Normans and high-minded Latin scholars, English has had to put up quite a fight. Yet, not only has the English language survived, it has also triumphed. The language of a small island rose to become the language of a Commonwealth, the conquering tongue of a myriad cultures and histories. Today English is recognized globally and spoken by millions as a first or second language; in fact there are more users of English as a first or second language, than any other language in the world.

So where should our story begin? It begins with the obscure dialects of the Germanic tribes (the Angles, the Saxons, the Frisii and the Jutes, among others) who settled in Britain during the fifth century, silencing the native tongue of the Celts and giving voice to a language that we now call Old English. Next came Roman missionaries, bringing with them manuscripts written in Latin. Such was their influence on not just religion but learning, that religious monasteries became places in which monks became fluent in reading and writing in Latin. It was only a matter of time before the monks turned their classical writing skills to their native tongue. By the seventh century, the simple runic alphabet used by the Celts and the early Saxons had been replaced by the first Old English alphabet – written English was born.

No one knows how many works in English were written at this time. The monasteries were often under attack by Viking invaders, forcing the monks to abandon them. When the Normans laid claim to England, English came to be regarded as the language of peasants and the preservation of Saxon writings would not have been high on the agenda of the new French king.

> There is only one surviving manuscript of the Old English epic poem *Beowulf*. Known as the Nowell Codex, it forms part of the British Library's Cotton Collection, and is held to be one of the most important works of Anglo-Saxon literature. Miraculously, it survived a fire in the eighteenth century.

The Norman Conquest did its best to smother Old English but, when it came to language skills, the Anglo-Saxons put on a show of resilience that the Normans failed to quash. Old English simply adapted and expanded, absorbing new words, forms and sound patterns until it evolved into the Middle English of the fourteenth and fifteenth centuries and the writings of such redoubtable authors as Geoffrey Chaucer, John Gower, William Langland, John Lydgate and Sir Thomas Malory.

William Caxton's printing press and the Renaissance period pushed the language still further forward into the Early Modern period, where Shakespeare's words echoed around the Globe Theatre. Finally, the Industrial Revolution and the age of Imperialism spread English around the world, giving rise to different dialects, creoles and conflicting vernaculars.

Any written history is, to some degree, defined as much by what it chooses to omit as it is by what it chooses to include. I am humble in comparison to the Venerable Bede, but nonetheless share the same dilemmas he would have had when composing his early chronicles of England. What to pass over and what to leave out? It seems absurd perhaps that a history of the English language could avoid anything but a passing mention of the achievements of Jane Austen, Charles Dickens or the Romantic poets. This is not due to any misplaced personal pride or prejudice, simply that the language of the nineteenth century differs comparatively little from the language of the twenty-first century, apart from matters concerning manners and style.

English has never been a static or stagnant language and in the twenty-first century it continues to flex its muscles, with English speakers and dictionary editors kept hard at work chasing its ever-changing vocabulary. While many of us may mourn once familiar words such as 'seldom', which are now seldom used, we have little choice but to embrace or adapt to the language of today. The invention of the Internet and mobile phones has created many new words for example, which have entered the vocabulary of the modern world. Some will soon be overtaken by advances in technology; others will be here to stay.

The future of English is unpredictable. Will Standard English stand the test of time against the international language of 'netspeak' or 'txt spk'? Or will this simplified form, so useful for ease and speed of communication and exchange, infiltrate and overtake?

Whatever happens in the future, the rich and unrivalled history of the English language deserves to be lauded, its story to be told.

JOSEPH PIERCY, 2012

PART ONE

—◦◦◦—

THE CELTS
AND THE
ROMANS

—◦◦◦—

(40 BC – AD 450)

Although the English language does not begin with the Celts, it is important to set the stage for its arrival. The Celts were Iron Age settlers to the British Isles, who migrated from central Europe from about 500 BC. By the time the Romans arrived in Britain the Celts were living as regional, warlike tribes. They were skilled farmers, potters and metal workers and were already known to be trading with the Roman colonies. Their craftsmen have left us evidence of intricately carved designs, but what of their language?

There is general agreement that a distinct Celtic language, separate from that of the Celtic tribes living in other parts of Europe, was spoken in Britain from around the middle of the first millennium BC up until the arrival of the Romans in the first century AD. The Celts left no written record of their history however, so we must depend on their contemporaries for enlightenment.

———෴———

Continental Celtic versus Insular Celtic

Early Greek and Roman scribes such as Herodotus (450 BC) and Polybius (200 BC) make reference to a loose ethnic grouping as the Keltoi or Galli in their written histories: a largely tribal society of warlike, iron-based communities. The similarity in stone inscriptions and artefacts discovered in Europe and Britain dating from this period points towards a form of shared language. The Keltoi described in the ancient Greek histories were the early Celts, dispersed as far south as the Iberian Peninsula and to the Scottish highlands in the north.

Although there are undoubted similarities between these tribal groups in terms of linguistic unity (e.g. alphabetical symbols and verb, subject, object word order), the chronicles of the ancient historians are contradictory and confusing. The Roman writer Tacitus stated that the language spoken by the Gauls was very similar to the language spoken by the early Britons. Julius Caesar, however, saw little similarity and noted that the three principal tribes of Gaul spoke in noticeably distinct dialects. As a result, to view the Celtic languages as belonging to one unified ethnic grouping is problematic, with modern historians preferring to divide the various dialects and forms into two distinct groups: Continental Celtic and Insular Celtic.

The first of these groupings, Continental Celtic, comprise Lepontic (spoken in the southern Alpine region), Celtiberian (spoken in parts of north-eastern Spain and Portugal), Gallaecian (north-western Spain and northern Portugal) and Gaulish (France and northern Alpine region). The second grouping, Insular Celtic, comprise two distinct linguistic families: Goidelic and Brythonic, which sub-divide into other related languages. The former (Goidelic) includes Irish and Scottish Gaelic and Manx and the later (Brythonic) Pictish and Cumbric (both extinct), British, Welsh, Breton and Cornish. As virtually all Continental Celtic is now extinct, exact geographical boundaries are a matter of vague approximation. In all probability, certain tribes were nomadic in aspect and this added to a crossing and merging of dialects, hence the conflicting views of Julius Caesar and Tacitus.

Linguistic researchers and historians have based the distinction between the two forms of Celtic on the hypothesis that the various forms spoken in the British Isles and Ireland evolved similar changes and innovations that don't appear prevalent in Continental Celtic. Insular Celtic verbs have different conjugational forms (verb endings) depending on where they appear in a sentence. For example, the Old Irish Celtic verb 'biru' in the first person singular means 'I carry'. The negative form however is represented by the conjunct 'ni biur' ('I do not carry') or, strictly speaking, 'not I carry'. This addition of a particle at the beginning of a sentence and the conjugated verb ending, appears to be a trait particular to the Insular Celtic family of languages and is not apparent in Continental Celtic, leading to the hypothesis that the Celtic languages of the British Isles, the earliest recorded tongue of our ancestors, evolved independently from the Celtic languages of Europe.

The Ogham Alphabet

The Celts left no written records to show us what their language looked like, although some coins exist with the names of Celtic leaders on them. Later literature incorporated inherited legends and histories from the time, but these endured due to the tradition of oral story-telling.

The Ogham Alphabet may be the closest we can get to what the writing of this time may have looked like. Traces of Ogham are found on around four hundred stone inscriptions and stone monuments dotted mostly around southern Ireland, Wales and the west of England (Devon and Cornwall).

Ogham is sometimes referred to as the Celtic Tree Alphabet as each of the twenty symbols corresponds to the name of a tree. The symbols themselves consist of a series of lines or slashes stemming out from or crossing a vertical line (like branches). The letters are grouped into four sets of five according to the point at which they cross or stem from the downward stroke or 'druim' (meaning 'spine'). Examples of vowels and consonants are:

	Letter	Name	Tree		Letter	Name	Tree
	B	Beith	birch		M	Muin	vine
	L	Luis	rowan		G	Gort	ivy
	D	Dair	oak		A	Ailm	silver fir
	C	Coll	hazel		I	Iodhadh	yew

The name 'Ogham' actually refers to the symbols themselves and the alphabet is more correctly known as the Beith Luis Nion alphabet. 'Beith' and 'Luis' are the first two letters and the letter 'nin', literally translated, means 'forked branch'.

Most examples of Ogham found on stone inscriptions date between the third and the sixth century, although these are the only surviving relics. It seems probable that the system existed earlier than these dates but that the symbols were carved on wood or other perishables.

There are various conflicting theories as to the reasons for the creation of the Ogham system. One much favoured by modern pagans and neo-occultists, is that it was designed as a secret language by Druids to transmit information in a form that could not be understood by the Romans when they invaded Britain. The system itself is not particularly complicated, however, and there are late Ogham inscriptions on stones that also contain Latin scripts, thereby suggesting that the secret code could be deciphered quite readily.

A second theory is that Ogham was developed by early Christian missionaries who settled in Ireland in the fourth century. The Latin-speaking Christians struggled to translate their own language into Old Irish and so needed a method of communicating short messages to the native speakers that could be easily understood.

Other Celtic scholars have proposed that the writing system was developed from a similar system used by Continental Druids in Gaul (France) in the sixth century, although modern dating techniques have placed some

Ogham inscriptions several centuries earlier. It is possible that Gaulish Druids had a secret system of hand signals and this accounts for the Ogham system being divided into four sets of five symbols (each stroke corresponding to the fingers).

Modern scholars have also suggested that Ogham was a primitive counting method as the symbols bear a passing resemblance to ancient tallying systems.

Although the origins or reasons for writing Ogham are unknown, the surviving examples carved into stones do little to elucidate the mystery. When translated, the majority of carvings appear to be names of people or places and were either used as boundary markers to divide territories or as memorials to the dead.

—◦◦◦—

The Roman Invasion

Julius Caesar led a largely exploratory army on to British shores in 55 BC and was met with some resistance from the Brythonic Celts, but it was a further hundred years before the Romans sent a serious invading force (an initial army of 40,000 centurions) in AD 43, under the decree of the Emperor Claudius. After once again meeting with some spirited resistance, the Roman army eventually overpowered the Celts and set up strongholds in southern England. Within three years, they had colonized most of the country. England remained under

Roman rule for the next four hundred years.

There is a tendency to view the term 'Empire' in a negative light, but in truth the Roman occupation had a civilizing effect upon the early Britons. Prior to Roman rule, the Celtic tribes were disparate and insular (and, I assume, fighting each other). Roman rule had a unifying effect as the tribes adopted Roman customs and laws and benefited from the social and technological advances the Romans brought with them. There is, however, one facet of the Roman conquest that remains an enigma: language.

Under the Romans, Latin became the 'official' language of the state and of governance, with numerous inscriptions on Roman ruins, public records and artefacts attesting to its widespread use. There is also evidence that native inhabitants from the higher social strata may have spoken Latin, or at least have been familiar enough with the language to use it when required.

The classical Roman historian Tacitus, in his history of the Roman general Agricola, writes of the native Celts embracing Roman Latin as a civilizing force. However, Tacitus may have been somewhat biased in his account as Agricola was his father-in-law.

The Romans, it seems, did not wish to force their language on to the native population. They saw their role as administrators and were happy to ignore the farming communities as long as they remained peaceful and complied with their demands. Undoubtedly, Celtic Britons would have understood Latin words in order to trade and complete business.

It would follow therefore, that early forms of Old English would be riddled with borrowings from the Latin spoken by the Romans. However, in actuality, the opposite is the case.

It is estimated that only two hundred Latin loan words are inherited from the Romans: a meagre return on almost four centuries of occupation. Of the words that have survived, or rather were incorporated into Old English from Roman Latin, most refer to place names of Roman settlements. The most notable examples of these are distortions of the original Roman names for cities, such as 'Londinium' (London), 'Lindum' (Lincoln), 'Cantabrigia' (Cambridge) and 'Dunelmum' (Durham). The names 'Britannia' for Great Britain and 'Caledonia' and 'Hibernia' for Scotland and Ireland date from the Roman occupation.

Other words which survived into Old English were coined by merchants and soldiers: 'win' (wine), 'candel' (candle), 'belt' (belt), 'stræt' (road) and 'weall' (wall).

There is a cruel irony, then, that the Brythonic Celtic tongue survived the Roman occupation and the cultural and social changes that went with it, but was in the end no match for the Germanic tribes who flocked to Britain after the Romans withdrew in AD 410.

PART TWO

—⁓—

THE RISE OF OLD ENGLISH

—⁓—

(AD 450 – 1066)

Angles, Saxons and Jutes

If, with the exception of the occasional uprising or period of insurrection, Roman Britain was relatively peaceful, the end of the Roman era ushered in a period of considerable upheaval for the Celtic tribes of Britain.

Left to defend themselves, they hired mercenaries to protect them from invaders, many of whom became a threat themselves, attracted by the rich farmland of the south and the east.

The historian Bede, writing at a later date, describes how the Celtic King Vortigern sent a request for help to a Germanic tribe (the Jutes, from Jutland, part of modern-day Denmark) who arrived in the year 449. The Jutes were employed as a mercenary army and successfully repelled the Scots and the Picts. As reward for their bravery and endeavours, Vortigern gave them the Isle of Thanet in Kent to settle in, believing that this would ensure their loyalty in case of further incursions from the north, as they would be protecting part of their own country. Unfortunately, Vortigern's plan backfired. The Jutes were quite taken with their newly acquired lands and consequently more and more Germanic tribes began to arrive from the Continent, including the Angles and the Saxons.

At first, the settlers may have lived side by side with the Celts, but as their numbers increased, this fragile alliance rapidly deteriorated. Bede writes that, 'they swarmed over the island and they began to increase so much that they became terrible to the natives themselves who had invited them'. The *Anglo-Saxon Chronicle* (an early Anglo-

Saxon history written in the time of Alfred the Great) lists a catalogue of bloody battles dating between 457 and 473 where the Germanic tribes massacred the Celts and forced them to flee their land. This process of domination, however, was probably more gradual than the *Chronicle* and Bede suggest.

The colonization of Britain by the Germanic tribes continued for a century and the Celtic tribes were forced further and further west into Cornwall, Wales and Cumbria and across the sea to Gaul (Brittany), taking their language and what remained of their civilization with them. Ultimately, this led to the near extinction of the Celtic language in many parts of Britain. It also led to the birth of the language known today as English.

Anglo-Saxons

In time, the various invading tribes settled into separate areas of England. Latin accounts of the period refer to the Germanic invaders as 'Saxones' and do not distinguish tribes or regions. It is assumed that they shared a common tongue, separated by minor shifts in dialect (much like English today).

In the eighth century, there were four main dialects: West Saxon, Mercian, Northumbrian and Kentish.

The Runic Alphabet

The Anglo-Saxons had a strong oral tradition but were probably illiterate. Some may have been familiar with Germanic runes, however – the letters in a set of alphabets used to write various Germanic languages. Old English initially made use of a version of this runic alphabet before adopting the Latin alphabet introduced by Christian missionaries.

Very few examples of Runic writing survive in manuscript form, although runic inscriptions can be seen on stones, jewellery and weapons.

The famous stone Anglo-Saxon cross known as the Ruthwell Cross (now in Dumfriesshire, Scotland) has writing in both Latin and the runic alphabet. The runic writing includes lines similar to the famous Old English poem 'The Dream of the Rood'.

Old English and Christianity

The rise of English and of the Christian Church is an interesting story. Christian missionaries arrived in Britain in the sixth century, gradually winning over the pagan population.

The earliest known Old English poem is 'Cædmon's Hymn', composed between 658 and 680. However, the poem was never written down by Cædmon himself. Cædmon was an illiterate Anglo-Saxon cowherd who looked after animals in a monastery. He was so inspired by his faith that he poured his feelings into songs. Bede recorded the words to 'Hymn' in Latin translation, but also noted Cædmon's 'poetical expressions of much sweetness and humility in English, which was his native language'.

Æthelbert (*c.* 560–616), the third king of Kent, was the first Saxon king to convert to Christianity. He had married Bertha, the Christian daughter of the king of the Franks – a powerful European state. Meanwhile, Pope Gregory I had for some time been set on converting the Britons, and in 597 he sent Augustine as a missionary from Rome.

Augustine landed on the Isle of Thanet in east Kent and shortly afterwards converted Æthelbert. Churches were established, and a wider-scale conversion to Christianity began. Monasteries were built and became seats of religious reflection and, more importantly for our story, of learning. The missionaries brought with them Latin manuscripts, and once again Roman Latin had a chance to make a stab at the native language. Latin was adopted as the language of religion and education, and devoted monks spent hours copying the manuscripts to add to monastery libraries.

The art of writing began to flourish – certainly in Latin. However, some scribes also chose to document secular stories such as the old legends of the Celts and some attempted to do this in their local dialect.

The exact date that Old English appeared as a written language is hard to pin down. For the most part, it was probably used for business purposes and legal matters. Æthelbert's law for Kent is thought to be the earliest example of a document written in Old English. It was probably written in the early seventh century and lists a system of fines.

England and 'English'

By the seventh century, the more common term for the inhabitants of England was Angli. In a letter written by Pope Gregory I, Æthelbert is addressed as 'rex Anglorum' or 'King of the Angles'. The language that the Angli (Angles) spoke seems to have been termed at an early stage as 'Anglisc'. Gradually, through a cross-fertilization of dialects, this word morphed into 'Englisc' (the 'sc' was pronounced 'sh'). It was not until the tenth century that the word 'Englaland' (place of the Angles) begins to appear in manuscripts and so, as far as historical evidence allows, scholars have deduced that the word 'English' for the language spoken by the early Anglo-Saxons predates the name England.

The Old English Alphabet

Old English was first written in runes (futhorc) but writers began to shift towards the script of the Latin alphabet introduced by Irish Christian missionaries.

The Old English Latin alphabet generally consisted of twenty-four letters, and was used from the ninth to the twelfth centuries. Twenty letters were taken from the Latin alphabet, two were adapted Latin letters (Æ, Ð), and two were from the runic alphabet (ᚷ, Þ). The letters K, Q and Z were not in use in native English words.

In the year 1011, a priest, monk and writer named Byrhtferð (c.970–c.1020) ordered the Old English alphabet for numerological purposes. He added an additional five English letters, resulting in a list of twenty-nine symbols:

A B C D E F G H I K L M N O P Q R S T V X Y Z and ᚷ Þ Ð Æ

Old English words were spelled as they sounded and the Latin alphabet sometimes had a struggle to represent this. Spellings varied widely as they were dependent on the writer's ear.

The Lindisfarne Gospels

One of the most prized works of its time was the Lindisfarne Gospels, a handwritten, illuminated manuscript, elaborately decorated and illustrated. It was produced between the late seventh and early eighth centuries at the Lindisfarne monastery on Holy Island, a small outcrop off the coast of Northumberland. The monastery was founded by the Irish monk Saint Aidan in 635, and established itself as the centre of Christian teaching in the north of England.

Illuminated manuscripts were labours of love and faith, designed to sanctify and celebrate the religious doctrines of the gospels and the word of God. Usually the projects were undertaken by groups of scribes and artists, but the Lindisfarne Gospels appears to have been the work of just one man, Eadfrith, Bishop of Lindisfarne. Eadfrith is thought to have begun the book in tribute to Saint Cuthbert, whose remains were buried on Holy Island in 698, to form the centrepiece of a shrine and promote Lindisfarne as a place of pilgrimage for early Anglo-Saxon Christians.

Some later records, most notably postscripts added to the text by Aldred (see below), state that Eadfrith, a prodigiously talented illustrator and scribe, took two years to complete the task with additional adornments added by skilled metal workers from the monastery.

The Lindisfarne Gospels is considered to be one of the finest surviving examples of Hiberno-Saxon or Insular art and a masterpiece of medieval book making.

The style mixes Celtic art, characterized by elaborate and intricate patterning of circles and spirals and markings common on Celtic stone crosses, with miniature ornate illustrations and iconography. The book also contains a huge range of colours used to decorate and gild the pages of the manuscript, a testament to the skills the monks had in producing and extracting subtle and vivid pigments from vegetable and animal matter. The completed text was covered in leather and fashioned with gemstones and fine metals and was probably used for ceremonial purposes at the monastery.

Towards the end of the eighth century, Lindisfarne suffered the first of many incursions by the Vikings. The Norse men ransacked the monastery and are believed to have pillaged the jewels and precious metals from the cover of the Gospels. After enduring further raids throughout most of the following century, the monks abandoned Lindisfarne in 875, taking with them the relics of St Cuthbert and the famous Gospels, finally settling in Chester Le Street, near Durham. It was at Chester le Street, a hundred years later, that a monk named Aldred added an Old English translation to the Gospels. Below the Latin lines of the original, Aldred painstakingly rendered the text, word by word, into the Anglo-Saxon language and added an important postscript testifying to its origins and author. Aldred's translation remains the oldest surviving version of the Gospels in English.

The legacy of the Lindisfarne Gospels lies not only in its importance as an ancient manuscript, but also as a beautiful work of art. It is often described as the oldest surviving work of art from the early medieval period, having somehow remained virtually intact through over a thousand years of strife and upheaval. Its translation for the native people, confirms that the Anglo-Saxons were no longer an illiterate people; English was gaining status.

The Campaign to Return the Gospels

Following the last Viking raid on Lindisfarne, the Gospels travelled far and wide, zealously protected by the Christian church. After Henry VIII dissolved the monasteries (around 1536), it is thought that the Gospels were seized and taken to London, where they were acquired by Sir Robert Cotton (1571–1631) for his library. The Cotton Library formed the basis for the newly established British Library in the eighteenth century and the Lindisfarne Gospels have remained in the library's hands ever since.

The 'ownership' of the Gospels remains a matter of bitter dispute, due to a vigorous campaign, supported by notable academics and politicians in North-East England, who believe the ancient manuscript should be returned to its rightful home in the region where it was created. The British Library is vehemently opposed to the campaign, but a compromise of sorts, after much wrangling, has been struck. The Gospels are 'loaned' every seven years, for a period of three months, to be put on public display in the North East.

Bede's *Ecclesiastical History of the English People*

Bede, an English monk (672/3–735), was a talented scholar, linguist, translator and author. His most famous work, *The Ecclesiastical History of the English People*, earned him the title 'The Father of English History'. Bede wrote most of his work in Latin, but his writings are hugely important as, for the first time, Britain's native population had its history written down.

So popular was Bede's history that, over a century later, and despite commissioning a history of his own, Alfred the Great had it translated into Anglo-Saxon.

—◦◦◦—

Viking Marauders: The Influence of Old Norse

Around 787, the first Viking incursions into Britain began. At first these raids were done seasonally and involved plundering as much as possible and then returning to various parts of Scandinavia before the onset of winter. However, by the middle of the ninth century, the Viking invaders began to establish settlements in the north and east of England, culminating under Alfred the Great with the establishment of the Danelaw, an area where Viking laws and customs held sway. During periods of relative peace, it was likely that more immigrants arrived from Danish and Norwegian tribes to settle in these areas.

Further Viking invasions in the early eleventh century brought more settlers into England and a short period of Viking rule during the exile of Æthelred the Unready and a succession of Danish kings. This relatively sustained contact with various Scandinavian groups over two centuries had a considerable effect on the Anglo-Saxon language.

The Vikings spoke a language known as Old Norse, which had similarities to Old English as they were both from the northern Germanic language tree. Old Norse contained various dialects, variants and sub-dialects (much as Old English had), but Old Norse is the linguistic term usually used to encompass tribespeople from modern-day Denmark, Norway and parts of Sweden, who settled in England during the Viking age.

Due to the similarities between the languages, it is possible that the two races could understand each other on a basic level and that, where new ideas were introduced (for example, through Christianity), words were loaned and swapped and new terms and expressions traded.

It is tempting to view the Viking age as characterized by bands of marauding Norsemen marching across the country engaged in seemingly endless conflicts and savagery. Although such occurrences were common and often terrible (it is estimated that the modern-day town of Carlisle in Cumbria remained abandoned and uninhabited for over a century, following a particularly vicious Viking raid), the periods of peace encouraged many Scandinavians to settle alongside their Anglo-Saxon counterparts – to integrate, trade with and inter-marry.

It is estimated that 1,400 loan words entered the English language during this period. Given the Viking's barbarous behaviour, it is fitting that the English words 'slaughter' (slátr), 'ransack' (rannsaka), 'anger' (angr) and 'die' (døyia) derive from Old Norse. However, other more benign words such as 'sister' (systir), 'husband' (húsbóndi), 'birth' (byrðr), and 'fellow' (félagi) hint at a more peaceful existence.

Many Viking settlers converted to Christianity and, with the exception of some specific Danish customs and laws observed during the period of the Danelaw, the two cultures were very similar, enabling naturalized Vikings to intergrate quite comfortably with their Anglo-Saxon neighbours. One area where the influence of the Scandinavian languages is particularly prevalent is in place names. Over a thousand place names in England are believed to have derived from Old Norse. Most notable are places ending with the suffix 'by', 'Derby', 'Rugby', 'Whitby' etc. The Danish word 'by' is taken to mean 'farm' or 'small town' and often this is preceded by a Nordic name. 'Whitby' therefore could have been 'Whit's farm' or 'a town founded by Whit'. Also common are place names ending in 'thorp' (meaning village) and 'toft' (a piece of land) as in 'Bishopsthorpe'

and 'Lowestoft'. A large percentage of these place names are concentrated in areas known to have been well-populated by Viking settlers, such as East Anglia, Yorkshire and Lincolnshire.

Another area where the influence of Scandinavian language is prominent is in the adoption of the patronymic 'son' in English personal names. The Old English variant was to add 'ing' as in 'Browning' and 'Downing', but areas where Old Norse was more prominent saw the use of 'son' in common present day names such as 'Johnson' and 'Stevenson', after the Nordic-style 'Svenson' (Sven's son).

It is estimated that there were about 25,000 words in the English language at this time and the Anglo-Saxons were hanging on to them. Just as they fought off the Viking threat, so they resisted Old Norse.

Alfred the Great

A lfred, the King of Wessex from 871 to 899, is the only English monarch to have been granted the sobriquet 'the Great'.

Supposedly, when Alfred was a child, he won a volume of English poetry, which his mother offered as a reward to the first of her children to be able to memorize it. Alfred had three elder brothers so was not expected to rule. If not physically strong, he was courageous and clever, and tales abound of his military acumen and fortitude in defeating the Vikings and in uniting the disparate Anglo-Saxon tribes. Other achievements often attributed to Alfred are creating the English navy, commissioning the *Anglo-Saxon Chronicle*, and founding Oxford University (and the burning of a few cakes along the way).

Although not all of the claims to Alfred's greatness can be adequately verified, it is certainly true that at the time of his succession to the throne of the Kingdom of Wessex, England was in grave danger of being conquered by the Vikings. The Anglo-Saxon kingdoms of Northumbria, Mercia and East Anglia were all under Viking control and Wessex, the last remaining province, only survived at first due to Alfred's diplomatic skills in brokering an uneasy peace agreement. It was not long before the Danes reneged on the treaty and attacked Alfred's army, pushing them back west into Dorset and Somerset. Alfred set about reorganizing his men and his strategy, and after engaging the help of local militia groups, set up an underground resistance movement that waged an effective guerrilla-style war against the Viking intruders.

In 878, Alfred launched a series of counter-attacks against the Danes, culminating in the Battle of Ethandun, where the Vikings were routed, retreated, and eventually surrendered. Guthrum, the Viking king, forged peace with Alfred, and under his guidance converted to Christianity.

Although further skirmishes with Viking tribes occurred throughout Alfred's reign (as they had done for many decades preceding him), the submission of Guthrum proved decisive in repelling the very real danger of a complete Viking invasion of England and ushered in a period of relative peace. As part of the peace treaty with Guthrum, East Anglia was granted to the Vikings to settle in (known as the Danelaw) and Alfred set about reclaiming the Kingdom of Mercia and, in particular, London.

Alfred's victory not only protected Anglo-Saxon Christianity from 'the Heathen Hordes', it also, in a very real sense, protected Old English from being swamped by Old Norse as the dominant tongue in the Middle Ages.

Alfred, so often portrayed as the great warrior king, is believed to have been slight in stature, learned and extremely pious. On surveying his new semi-united kingdoms, Alfred recognized the damage that the Vikings had exacted on Christian culture and learning. The persistent ransacking and burning of monasteries had robbed the Church of many invaluable manuscripts and teachings. There was simply nowhere for priests to be trained to impart the values of Christianity to the masses, and clergymen well versed in Latin and the rigours of scholarship were in sharp decline.

To remedy what he perceived to be a spiritual vacuum, Alfred embarked on a programme of radical reform. Now aged forty, he taught himself Latin and enlisted the help of noted scholars from Europe to oversee the translation of key texts from Latin into Old English, 'books of wisdom most necessary for all men to know'. Alfred's quest was two-fold. As he writes in the preface to his translation of Pope Gregory's *Pastoral Care*, his principal aim was 'to set to learning all the free-born young men now in England who have the means to apply themselves to it'.

However, literacy was scarce in English, let alone Latin, even amongst the noble classes. In order that his people might 'apply themselves to it', Alfred set up court-sponsored schools and centres for the less privileged to promote reading and writing in English, with initial instruction to be undertaken in the native tongue. Those who showed aptitude were to continue further studies in Latin. The copies of the translations Alfred commissioned were sent out to the Bishops of the twelve Christian diocese with instructions to impart the spiritual teachings in a language that the people could embrace and understand.

The traditions of scholarship were revived in the monasteries and Winchester was established as not only the royal capital, but as a centre of spiritual and cultural learning. Through seeking to restore spiritual values and codes to his ravaged and oppressed subjects, Alfred succeeded in preserving and promoting Old English, a language, particularly in written form, that might have faced extinction, given that the Danes had a reputation for burning manuscripts.

The *Anglo-Saxon Chronicle*

The *Anglo-Saxon Chronicle* is one of the most important documents to be written in English. It is thought that it was compiled on the orders of Alfred the Great in approximately 890 as a tool to promote scholarship and to strengthen the identity of the Anglo-Saxons. It was continuously updated so that it details the history of England from the Roman invasion up to the Norman conquest.

Although the *Chronicle* is neither a complete history of this period, nor fully trustworthy, without it, and Bede's account, we would have no record of what happened in Britain during these years.

The original chronicle, compiled by monastery scribes, was copied and distributed to other monasteries around the country, where other monks and scribes took on the job of revising and updating it – often giving precedence to local events, so that actually the histories began to differ.

The earliest manuscript that can be dated is The Winchester Chronicle, which was written by monastery scribes and was completed in 893. Nine manuscripts survive, all of which are copies, and these were geographically spread across the country from Peterborough in the north, to Worcester in the west and Canterbury in the east. Seven of the surviving versions of the Chronicle are written in Old English. One, the Canterbury Chronicle, is written in Old English and Latin, and the last, which was written at Peterborough at the end of the twelfth century, was written in Middle English. In this respect, the chronicles are also of importance as early examples of written English in its various forms, with the Peterborough Chronicle representing the oldest surviving manuscript written in early Middle English.

The feminine pronoun 'scæ' (she) is first recorded in the Peterborough Chronicle.

The Riddles of the Exeter Book

Of all the surviving manuscripts in Old English, perhaps the most curious is the Exeter Book – a miscellany of poems, maxims and riddles, loosely arranged to form an anthology. As with most literature of the time, the author (or authors) remains anonymous, but it is generally considered to have been the work of monastic scribes in the west of England.

The book itself is believed to date from between 960 and 990, but some of its contents may date to much earlier. It is first mentioned in the papers of Leofric, the first Bishop of Exeter and consul of Edward the Confessor. Leofric was an avid collector of manuscripts and on taking up the post of Bishop at Exeter in 1050, he was dismayed to find that his new cathedral contained barely a handful of books.

Leofric set about building a library in the cathedral with the aim of making Exeter a centre of scholarship. On his death in 1072, the cathedral catalogue lists over sixty books bequeathed to the library by Leofric. Among them was 'a large English book of poetic works about all sorts of things'.

Alongside versions of popular poems of the age such as 'The Wanderer', 'The Seafarer' and 'The Wife's Lament' are maxims relating to the scriptures and ninety-five riddles, cryptically written in poetic form. The origins of the practice of riddling developed from missionaries coming to England from the Continent. There was a tradition of composing riddles in Latin dating back to the author Symphosius in the fourth century and his collection of one hundred riddles, commonly known as the *Aenigmata* (the origin of the word 'enigmatic').

Aldhelm, the colourful Abbott of Malmesbury, composed a collection of one hundred Latin riddles in the late seventh century. The Exeter Book contains ninety-five riddles, leading scholars to the conclusion that some may have been lost (the fact that several pages of the manuscript are singed, attests to various attempts to burn it through the ages). The Exeter riddles are unique in that they are longer, self-contained poems, whereas the traditional Latin riddles consisted of three lines giving clues to their solutions (the solution is usually given in the title).

For example:

Anchor

My twin points are bound by an iron bar.
I wrestle with wind, struggle with the sea.
I probe deep waters – I bite the earth.

RIDDLE 13, THE AENIGMATA, SYMPHOSIUS

I must fight with the waves whipped up by the wind,
grapple alone with their force combined,
when I dive to earth under the sea.
My own country is unknown to me.
If I can stay still, I'm strong in the fray;
If not, their might is greater than mine,
they'll break me in fragments and put me to flight,
meaning to wreck what I must protect.
I can foil them if my fins are not frail,
and the rocks hold firm against my force.
You know my nature, now guess my name?

RIDDLE 16, THE EXETER BOOK

The Latin riddle of Symphosius is prefaced by the solution ('anchor'), whereas the Exeter riddle is more playful, teasing the reader to find the answer. The use of personification is also much more self-conscious in the Old English riddle, describing the anchor dropped in the heat of battle, fighting against both the elements of wind and sea and alluding to the need to hold firm during a possible sea skirmish (sea battles were conducted by dropping anchor next to the enemy boat, lashing the two boats together and conducting hand to hand combat on a floating platform).

Many of the riddles describe the natural world in metaphorical terms, transposing animals and their habits to everyday objects. Several of the riddles use bawdy sexual imagery and double entendres to effect their disguise. The following description of a helmet being a case in point:

> A lovely woman, a lady, often locked me
> in a chest; at times she took me out
> with her fingers, and gave me to her lord
> and loyal master, just as he asked.
> Then he poked his head inside me,
> pushed it up until it fitted tightly.
> I, adorned, was bound to be filled
> with something rough if the loyal lord
> could keep it up. Guess what I mean?
>
> RIDDLE 61

In contrast to the riddles, the poems 'The Wanderer' and 'The Seafarer' do not make for cheerful reading. Instead, they evoke a haunting sense of desolation and loneliness, of separation from loved ones, of the misery of exile, and the terrors of the sea. They are poems of forbearance, of the hardships of life endured with God's help. They are the voice of our ancestors, speaking to us across centuries. That is, if we can understand them:

Mæg ic be me sylfum	I can make a true song
soðgied wrecan	about me myself
siþas secgan	tell my travels
hu ic geswincdagum	how I often endured
earfoðhwile	days of struggle
oft þrowade	troublesome times
bitre breostceare	[how I] have suffered
gebiden hæbbe	grim sorrow at heart

In 1602, the Dean and Chapter of Exeter Cathedral presented a number of their most precious texts to the newly founded Bodleian Library, but left the Exeter Book behind. Perhaps they did not realize the significance of this wonderful collection of Old English poetry; it is probable they could not read it.

—⟡⟡⟡—

The Barmy Abbot of Malmesbury

Aldhelm was a leading seventh-century clergyman, Latin poet and scholar, who held the post of Abbot of Malmesbury for thirty years before becoming Bishop of Sherborne. Aldhelm wrote most of his works in extremely flowery and grandiloquent Latin and was fond of composing Latin riddles. Some contemporary accounts claim he also wrote Old English poetry and riddles, leading some scholars to suggest Aldhelm as the author of some of the Exeter Book riddles. Something of an eccentric, Aldhelm is said to have often dressed in outlandish, clown-like clothes and encouraged people into his churches by wandering the streets singing songs and reciting poems and scripture readings, many of which he had put to music. Passing reference to Aldhelm's songs is made in the *Anglo-Saxon Chronicle*, suggesting they were still popular in the tenth century, although no copies of them have survived.

Beowulf

In the introduction to his book *The Seven Basic Plots*, writer and critic Christopher Booker draws a comparison between *Beowulf* and the 1970s blockbuster *Jaws*. Booker's thesis is that only seven stories exist and that they are told and retold in different forms, across time and place and cultural boundaries. It is a seductive idea.

On a basic level, the comparisons between *Jaws* and *Beowulf* are self-evident in that both stories concern a community terrorized by a monster (in the case of *Beowulf*, three separate monsters) and feature a hero who defeats the tyrant (often against the odds) and saves the people. The 'Overcoming the Monster' narrative that Booker identifies appears in the popular mythology of many ancient cultures and civilizations. In *Beowulf* it appears in written English for the first time.

The story of the adventures of Beowulf, a warrior king of Scandinavia, is told in the form of an epic poem of over three thousand alliterative lines. Only one surviving copy of the original text survives and is believed to date sometime between the eighth and eleventh centuries. This manuscript was composed anonymously, but appears to have been written by two different scribes.

The composition of the poem has been the subject of much scholarly study and debate, with various theories proposed and rejected. One common idea is that because it is structured in alliterative verses, the poem was passed down from an oral tradition and that poets performed it for entertainment purposes. The alliterative style was therefore designed to make the poem (story) easier to remember. Possibly, the *Beowulf* scribes were merely transcribing performances of the poem (many of which may have differed with various additions, embellishments and improvisations) and arranging the story into a cohesive text or record.

The narrative can be divided into three distinct parts structured around Beowulf's battles. In the first part Hroogar (or Hrothgar), King of the Danes, builds a large mead hall named Heorot (a form of medieval court/pub where much feasting and drinking occurred). The noisy celebrations, and particularly the singing, enrage the sensibilities of Grendel, a troll living in a nearby swamp. Grendel attacks Heorot at night and kills and eats several of Hroogar's men. Terrorized by Grendel and helpless to defend themselves, Hroogar and his men leave their court. Beowulf, learning of Hroogar's plight, arrives with a band of men and offers to kill Grendel. Beowulf and his warriors wait in Heorot for Grendel to attack and, after an epic battle, Beowulf slays Grendel by ripping off his arm, whereupon Grendel runs off to his swamp to die.

The second section of the narrative concerns the battle with Grendel's mother, who attacks Heorot in revenge for Grendel's death. Beowulf and his warriors follow Grendel's mother to her lair in a cave below a lake, whereupon Beowulf swims to the bottom of the lake and, after another titanic fight (and a fair slice of good fortune), he kills Grendel's mother with a magic sword he finds in the cave. In honour of his heroic deeds, Beowulf is made king of his people and he reigns in peace and prosperity for fifty years.

The final part of the poem concerns Beowulf's battle with a terrible fire-breathing dragon who awakes from a long sleep to terrorize Beowulf's kingdom. Beowulf is an old man but, donning his armour for one last adventure, he hunts down the dragon with the help of Wiglaf, a young warrior. (After an early skirmish, the rest of Beowulf's men no longer had much stomach for the fight.) Beowulf and Wiglaf eventually destroy the dragon, but the effort takes its toll on Beowulf, who returns to his people carrying a mortal wound and dies (but not before naming Wiglaf as his successor).

So is, as Christopher Booker suggests, *Beowulf* 'important as it shows an age-old, timeless myth rendered into written form by a developing language', or is it important in other senses also? The fact that *Beowulf* is a poem is key in this respect. A language has to have confidence in itself and to display elements of self-consciousness to develop poetic forms. Seamus Heaney, the Nobel Prize-winning Irish poet, has produced one of the most memorable and successful translations of *Beowulf* in modern English. In the introduction to his version, Heaney speaks of 'the melancholy and fortitude' of the poetry, the strange word choices and wonderful synonyms and compound words, coming to the conclusion that the poet (or poets) of *Beowulf* had a mastery of their language and the 'self-consciousness of an artist convinced we must labour to be beautiful'.

Heaney also points to the wide vocabulary displayed in the poem, with words created to fit the mythology and to imagine the unimaginable, as evidence that Old English was a playful and creative language. For example, boats are described as 'wave steeds' and the human body as a 'ban hus' (bone-house). *Beowulf* is rich and lavish with figurative synonyms and compounds known as 'kennings'. Kennings are words used to describe things in oblique or poetic ways. Old English has around fifty recorded words for the sea in various forms, ranging from 'seolh bæp' (seal-bath) to 'fisces eðel' (fishes home) and 'hwæl weg' (whale-way) many of which appear only in *Beowulf*. It is unclear if there were any specific conventions for the usage of one figurative description over another, but it seems likely it was a poetic embellishment to fit the alliterative style of the poem. The tone and form are fixed from the very first line:

> Hweat, we Gar-Dena in geardagum
> How, the Spear-Danes in days of yore

The 'Gar-Dena' (Spear-Danes) are the tribe of King Hroogar but are described in various different ways throughout the poem including, 'Scyldings' and 'Beorht-Denes' (Bright Danes), usually to satisfy the alliterative structure.

Beowulf, along with other Old English texts such as 'The Wanderer' and 'The Seafarer', represents the body of classical Anglo-Saxon literature and provides valuable insight into the vivid descriptive style of Old English and the prevailing culture of the time.

PART THREE

MIDDLE ENGLISH: GEOFFREY CHAUCER AND ALL THAT

(1066 – 1475)

A Language United?

'Language is power,
life and the instrument of culture,
the instrument of domination and liberation'
ANGELA CARTER,
ENGLISH NOVELIST AND ESSAYIST (1940-92)

After King Alfred unified the diverse Anglo-Saxon kingdoms in 878, there was a marked decline in the significance of regional dialects. Although they still existed, the majority of written materials which date from the Anglo-Saxon period are written in the dialect of Alfred's kingdom, Wessex. In order to govern the various regions, a standardized language needed to be employed; and what better language than that of the ruling party?

Alfred's drive to spread literature around the country was also a powerful ploy to establish his brand of English, as well as to better establish a sense of identity and permanence among Anglo-Saxons. Peace was short-lived, however, with more Viking attacks on their way. In 1017, the Viking king Cnut was accepted as king of all England – and remained so for twenty years. The invaders from the North were finally in check, and the French were hovering just over the Channel.

Are You Shore You Meant That?

King Canute (or Cnut) has become famous for his foolish and arrogant attempt to hold back the tide. This story was first recorded in Henry of Huntingdon's twelfth-century chronicle of the history of England. However, the account was meant to flatter the king, who was said to be tired of his fawning courtiers and was trying to demonstrate that a king is not all-powerful. The story may well be apocryphal.

> ... Somme can Frensche and no Latyn
> That used han cowrt and dwellen therein
> And somme can of Latyn a party
> That can of Frensche but feebly
> And somme vnderstonde wel Englysch
> That can nother Latyn nor Frankys
> Bothe lered and lewed, olde and yonge
> Alle vnderstonden english tonge.
> WILLIAM OF NASSYNGTON, 1325

The defeat of Harold Godwinson at the Battle of Hastings threatened to destroy the English language. Norman noblemen assumed positions of power and authority and Old English was relegated to a position of subservience below French. Although English was to resist and eventually rise and prosper, profound changes occurred to the language. The complicated grammar of Old English with its inflections and cases fell away and changes to the pronunciation of vowels occurred. Yet, amid all the political upheaval, English held on, in vernacular Bible translations, in business matters, in law and in literature.

What was very interesting was that after the Norman Conquest English became nothing but a 'patois' (a peasant language without a writing system). Old English was pretty well standardized, but after 1066 all standardization disappeared and what you had was dialects.   J. H. FISHER, MEDIEVALIST

The Domesday Book

William the Conqueror was crowned on Christmas Day in 1066. The coronation took place at Westminster Abbey and was conducted in both Latin and English, though the new king spoke in French throughout the ceremony. As King Alfred had set himself the task of learning Latin, aged forty, so William made an attempt to learn English, aged forty-three. However, it would appear that he soon gave it up.

Instead he set about securing his newly acquired

kingdom through the forced acquisition of land. French noblemen arrived, and loyal knights who had supported him during the invasion were rewarded with land – on which they built strategically placed, imposing stone castles. Some English noblemen who swore allegiance to William were also rewarded to avoid any potential backlash against the Norman invaders. Around a quarter of the land in England was owned by the Crown, a further quarter given over to the Church (which was a necessary pay-off as the Church in Rome had officially sanctioned the invasion) and the rest was divided up between the new aristocracy.

In 1085, William summoned a group of his counsellors and ordered that a wide-ranging land survey be undertaken. The purpose of this audit was two-fold. Principally, it was to form a concise and detailed record of who owned what for the purpose of taxation – or more specifically, the raising of Danegeld, a tax levied on the subjects of England to pay for the defence of the realm or to quash any possible civil insurgency. It also provided William with a neat method and apparatus to ensure that no single landowner was able to call upon the necessary financial resources to mount an effective challenge to his authority. The *Anglo-Saxon Chronicle* describes the bureaucratic diligence of the survey in less than glowing terms:

> So very narrowly, indeed, did he commission them to trace it out, that there was not one single hide, nor a yard of land, nay, moreover (it is shameful to tell,

though he thought it no shame to do it), not even an ox, nor a cow, nor a swine was there left, that was not set down in his writ. And all the recorded particulars were afterwards brought to him.

The Domesday Book actually comprises two separate surveys, Little Domesday, which covered the east of England (Norfolk, Suffolk and Essex), and Great Domesday, which assessed the rest of England and areas of Wales, with a few notable omissions: the principal cities of Winchester and London and areas in the north of England, such as Durham, which had been granted their own taxation rights. The 'books' themselves were handwritten in Latin on to sheepskin parchments in black and red ink, with both volumes running to over four hundred leaves. Despite its name, Little Domesday is actually the longest volume, suggesting that the Great Domesday survey wasn't completed, either because of William's death or because the whole venture became too complex.

Although written in a short form of Latin, the text contains some examples of vernacular Anglo-Saxon English, mostly in the form of personal names, place names and specific elements for which there was no obvious Latin equivalent. Overall, the Domesday Book is a document that provides historians with invaluable information about the social and economic situation in England in the early decades after the Norman invasion.

Why Was the Domesday Book So Called?

The name 'Domesday Book' was not coined by the Normans, who called their survey 'The Book of Winchester' – the records being held in the treasury office in Hampshire. In 1179, Richard FitzNeal, exchequer to King Henry II' wrote: 'This book is called by the native English Domesday, that is Day of Judgement . . . for as the sentence of that strict and terrible last account cannot be evaded by any skilful subterfuge, so when this book is appealed to . . . its sentence cannot be put quashed or set aside with impunity. That is why we have called the book The Book of Judgement' . . . because its decisions, like those of the Last Judgement, are unalterable.' (*Dialogus de Scaccario*). The pronunciation of the time being different from now, 'dome' was pronounced 'doom'.

Norman French: The Language of Class and Culture

William I set about installing Normans into positions of power and influence across all areas of English life. The Anglo-Saxon aristocracy was effectively replaced and by 1075, all twelve of the Earls of England were Normans. A similar situation occurred with the clergy. Only one bishop, Wulfstan of Worcester, was native English, and his influence upon the court was limited. Wulfstan was denied the right to act as counsel to the King by the Norman Archbishop of Canterbury, Leofranc, on the grounds that he (Wulfstan) couldn't speak French and was therefore an ignoramus.

By the reign of Henry I, in the early decades of the twelfth century, the historian monk William of Malmesbury observed: 'No Englishman today is an Earl or Bishop or Abbot. The newcomers gnaw at the wealth and guts of England, nor is there any hope of ending this misery'.

The abundance of Norman aristocrats ensured that the wealthy and the landed gentry all spoke French. Latin was used for legal purposes and church ceremonies. In 1154, the monks abandoned their work on the *Anglo-Saxon Chronicle*.

English remained the spoken language of the masses, the peasants, the serfs and the people in rural areas, but the native language became very much an indicator of class status. Gradually, through inter-marriage and the co-existence of the two languages, the Norman nobility would have developed some understanding of English, even if they deigned not to speak it. Likewise, through commerce and trade, members of the English-speaking lower and middle classes would undoubtedly have had some grasp of Norman French. The degree to which England was a bilingual society is difficult to measure. Matters of importance were documented in French or Latin – but the health of English was not one of these.

The Middle-English Creole Hypothesis

The radical differences between Old English and Middle English has proved a rich area for academic study and debate. In the 1950s, historical linguists became interested in looking at creole languages, tracing their roots and proposing theories examining their formation. The traditional view had been to regard creoles as inferior, bastardized versions of two or more parent languages that were spoken by uncivilized and uncultured populations. Contemporary linguistic studies promote a different view, one which puts forward the idea that creoles are not merely over-simplified hybridizations of other languages but are, in a sense, new languages born from mixing previously existing forms.

Typically, a creole language is formed from a pidgin language. Pidgins are the mixing of two or more parent languages into a base language as a means of communication for two distinct communities or groups who do not share a common tongue. In 1977, the linguists Charles Bailey and Karl Maroldt developed the theory that Middle English was a creole language and this explains the vast difference between Middle English and Old English. The theory takes as a central premise the notion that forty per cent of Middle English in terms of lexicon, phonology and semantics, is a mixture of Old French, Middle French and Anglo-Saxon (Old) English, with some added garnishing from Old Norse. The regular Viking incursions and the

Norman conquest are taken as the major factors in the creolization of Old English.

Old English was a highly inflected language containing an elaborate system of declension for nouns, conjugation of verbs and five grammatical cases. These linguistic structures were either lost or simplified between the eleventh and fifteenth centuries. Nouns, for example, cases now had just two, regular and genitive and many verb structures were no longer conjugated (changed according to different aspects).

The Middle-English Creole Hypothesis divided scholars into two distinct camps. On one hand it is irrefutable that dramatic changes in the form and structure of the native language took place in the period of transition from Old to Middle English. The numerous French loan words adopted into the English lexicon and the sharing of word stems suggests a process of hybridization of pre-existing linguistic forms. Under Norman rule, Latin and French (Anglo-Norman) were the official languages used in public ceremonies and for governance and law, but Anglo-Saxon was the language spoken by the majority of the population outside the Royal Court and higher echelons of the nobility.

Other scholars, such as Anthony Warner, have pointed to church sermons and Bible translations as proof that England at this time was principally a trilingual country, with many people comfortable with and able to understand Latin, French and English. In this sense then, to what extent is Middle English a true creole language if pre-existing languages were used side by side?

The common view among academics is that rather than the influences of other languages 'killing' Old English, the prevailing melting pot of different linguistic forms helped to enrich the English language. As the use of Anglo-Norman and Latin started to diminish towards the end of the fourteenth century, English emerged and evolved to become the dominant tongue, having absorbed other aspects during an era of linguistic instability.

—◦◊◦—

The *Ormulum*

One of the most important surviving written relics from the Early Middle English period can be found in the Bodleian Library in Oxford: the *Ormulum*.

The *Ormulum* manuscript was probably written between 1150 and 1180, by a monk named Orm (or Ormin), from Bourne Abbey in Lincolnshire. It is largely composed of homilies (commentaries on the scriptures) and it is thought that these were intended to be read out in church services. Church services were still conducted in Latin, by French-speaking priests, and thus were largely unintelligible to ordinary English-speaking people. Orm's translations acted as a bridge between the priests and their congregations.

The significance of the *Ormulum* lies neither in its importance as a work of biblical exegesis, nor in its considerable artistic power and merit. Rather, it lies in the creation of a unique orthography. Facing the problem of a language that was fragmenting, Orm clearly intended to try to preserve or standardize the spellings of the English words he used. He devised a system to distinguish between short and long vowels. Words containing short vowels in closed syllables were spelt with double consonants after the vowel, long vowels with single consonants.

Forrþrihht anan se time comm
þatt ure Drihhtin wollde
ben borenn i þiss middellærd
forr all mannkinne nede

As soon as the time came
that our Lord wanted
to be born in this middle-earth
for the sake of all mankind.

Orm seems to have been particularly pleased with his system. At one point in his manuscript, he added a note requesting that any future scribes copying his work should be mindful of the correct spelling of words.

We don't know how many copies were made, but only one copy of Orm's manuscript exists today. It was not until 1400 that Middle English began to adopt a standard form. However, Orm's efforts have proved immensely helpful to contemporary scholars trying to grapple with the pronunciation of Early Middle English.

Twitter and Tweets: *The Owl and the Nightingale*

Dahet habbe that ilke best
that fuleþ his owe nest.

Ill fortune take that thing unblest,
The bird who fouls his own nest.

The Middle English poem *The Owl and the Nightingale* is believed to have been very popular in its time. It is written in the form of a debate between the two birds of the title. The poem is approximately 2,000 lines long; the birds had a lot to say. It may have written between 1189 and 1216 by one Nicholas of Guildford.

Wycliffe's Bible

John Wycliffe (1328–1384) was a prominent Oxford scholar, preacher and theologian credited with overseeing the first full-length translation of the Bible into the English language. By the middle of the fourteenth century, the only access the population had to the Bible was through readings and scriptures in church services. Literacy levels were low and few people were significantly versed in Latin to be able to study the Bible. The Latin Vulgate Bible was considered to be sacred by the Catholic Church; indeed, to produce translations of the Bible without the express consent of the Roman Catholic Church in Rome was considered to be an act of heresy.

Wycliffe and his followers were disenchanted with the Church, believing it had been corrupted by its wealth and power. For Wycliffe, all Christian teaching started and ended with the Bible and he believed that everyone should have access to it in their own language.

To this end, Wycliffe put together a team of translators, including Nicholas of Hereford, and the church reformer John Purvey. Each translator took a different portion of the Vulgate and, following a strict word order, rendered the sacred text into a Middle English vernacular.

Once the translation had been completed, Wycliffe needed to circulate it. He began to train a select band of lay preachers, who made many copies of Wycliffe's Bible and travelled around the country preaching to the common people in rural areas and small towns. This underground movement called itself the Christian Brethren and was committed to reforming the Church by taxing its wealth and taking away the authority bestowed upon the priesthood.

Initially the Catholic Church seemed to tolerate Wycliffe's Bible and the fact that several hundred copies have survived to the present day suggests the Christian Brethren were successful in their endeavours. Wycliffe's followers became known as 'Lollards' (a somewhat dismissive term taken to mean 'mumblers') and were in effect forerunners of the later Reformation movement.

Eventually, however, the Church intervened, worried that Wycliffe's followers represented a genuine threat to their authority. Wycliffe was accused (inaccurately) of involvement in the Peasants' Revolt of 1381, dismissed from his academic post at Oxford University and branded a heretic.

John Wycliffe died after suffering a stroke in 1384. The persecution of his followers continued through the last decades of the fourteenth century and into the early part of the fifteenth century. In 1401, the first of a series of Church statutes was passed, banning Wycliffe's writings and stating that the translation of Bible scriptures by lay preachers was an act of heresy. The Lollards were forced into hiding, many were pursued, tried and burnt at the stake. 'The Council of Constance', a religious court set up to tackle any affront to Church authority, declared Wycliffe a heretic, and ordered that his body be exhumed.

In 1428, on the orders of Pope Martin V, Wycliffe's grave in Lutterworth was ransacked by priests, his bones dug up and ceremonially burned, his ashes deposited in a nearby river.

Although Wycliffe's stated intention was to make the Bible more accessible to English people, the method of his translation made this problematic. By following the Vulgate Bible so closely, a large number of Latin words found their way into the English version. It is estimated that over a thousand words of Latin derivation were recorded for the first time in written English in Wycliffe's Bible, and transliterated by its readers into common idiom.

Common expressions such as 'woe is me' and 'an eye for an eye' appear for the first time in Wycliffe's Bible. The Lollards may have ultimately been defeated in their aims, persecuted and martyred for their beliefs, yet the survival of so many copies of Wycliffe's Bible, in the face of stringent censorship and wholesale book burning, is a testament to its historical importance.

—⟨ɞ⟩—

Chaucer and *The Canterbury Tales*

In Southwark at the Tabard as I lay
Redy to wenden on my pilgrymage
To Canterbury with ful devout corage,
At nyght was come into that hostelrye
Wel nyne and twenty in a compaignye
Of sundry folk, by aventure yfalle
In felaweshipe, and pilgrims were they alle,
That toward Canterbury wolden ryde.

Geoffrey Chaucer is often described as the Father of English Literature and the principal poet of the high Middle Ages. Born in London around 1343, Chaucer was the son of a prominent wine merchant, John Chaucer, who inherited a profitable vintners business through marriage. At the age of fourteen, probably through his father's business connections with the London nobility, Chaucer was sent to be a page to the Duke of Clarence. This led to Chaucer embarking on a long career as a public servant in a variety of different roles around the royal courts of Edward III and Richard II and, as a result, court papers from the period have provided historians with a wealth of information about Chaucer's professional life.

In 1359, Chaucer served with his patron the Duke of Clarence in the Hundred Years War and undertook various diplomatic missions, travelling to France, Spain and, most significantly, Italy. It was on one of many trips to Italy during the 1370s, that Chaucer encountered the work of writers Boccaccio and Petrarch, which may have sparked his interest in classical poetry. There are certainly noticeable similarities between Boccaccio's *Decameron* and Chaucer's most famous work *The Canterbury Tales*.

Chaucer's first work, *The Book of The Duchess,* was written to commemorate the death of Blanche of Lancaster, the wife of Edward III's son, John of Gaunt. Four dreadful plagues devastated England in Chaucer's lifetime and, in 1369, Queen Philippa and her daughter-in-law Blanche succumbed to the third of these. Unlike his father, who had little time for the English language, John of Gaunt encouraged it. He is thought to have commissioned Chaucer to write the poem.

The term 'parliament' dates from 1236, when King John was forced to allow commoners ('commons') among his advisers. 'Parliament' comes from the French *parler*, which means to talk or to discuss. In 1360, parliament passed a bill, introduced by John of Gaunt, making English the official language of the Law Courts.

In 1374, Chaucer took up the post of Comptroller of the London Port Authority and it is thought that the majority of his works were written during the twelve-year period of his tenure at the customs office. On St George's Day of that year, court records show that King Edward III decreed that Chaucer be awarded a gallon of wine for every day of his life. Although it is unclear why the King passed this edict, it was traditional for the monarch to reward artists on saints' days and, given Chaucer had written an elegy for the King's deceased daughter-in-law, the suggestion is that Chaucer was regarded as an unofficial court poet alongside his administrative duties.

When, two centuries later, James I established the office of the Poet Laureate, he paid Ben Jonson in wine, thereby reviving a tradition established in Chaucer's time.

The Canterbury Tales marks a radical departure from Chaucer's earlier poetry. Works such as *Troilus and Criseyde* and *The Book of The Duchess* draw upon classical mythology for their sources and very much reflect the vogue for a genre known as courtly romances. *The Canterbury Tales* was innovative in relation to the literature of the time through its use of a naturalized setting. The story concerns a group of pilgrims on their way to visit the relics of Saint Thomas Becket in Canterbury Cathedral. To entertain themselves on their journey they have a storytelling competition, with the winner awarded free food. The group is a motley crew covering the different classes of medieval society, from knights and parsons down to cooks and millers. In the 'General Prologue', Chaucer introduces and describes each of the pilgrims as they gather at an inn prior to embarking on their journey and sets up the framework for the storytelling competition. Lots are drawn to determine who tells the first tale and the knight wins the honour. The narrator (taken to be Chaucer) explains to the reader that the order of the tales should proceed 'by degree' (i.e. according to social class and status) but interestingly, this proposed structure is abandoned early on, when at the end of the knight's tale, the drunken miller interrupts to tell his tale.

The contrasts between the tales in terms of genre, style and language is often quite marked, on account of Chaucer allowing his pilgrims to tell their tales in their own words. 'The Knight's Tale' draws upon a tragic story of two knights who both fall in love with the same princess and reflects the courtly romance genre for classical tales of chivalry. The knight, in recounting his tale, peppers it with grand descriptions of wealth, power and status and the vocabulary he uses is unambiguous, simple and correct. Taking up the theme of two men desiring the same woman, the miller responds with a coarse tale about the flighty young wife of a hapless ageing carpenter being pursued by two predatory younger men. The miller colours his tale with bawdy humour and bodily functions to great comedic effect, and although the tale is told in an almost deadpan fashion, with one event quickly following another, the plot is actually far more complex.

In essence, 'The Miller's Tale' is a fabliau, a comic poem made up by court jesters, which usually revolved around sexual subject matter and often contained an elaborate confidence trick (in this case a convoluted ruse to get the carpenter's wife into bed). The fabliau was very popular in European courts in the thirteenth and fourteenth centuries and Chaucer would have been familiar with the form on account of his diplomatic travels.

The drunken miller, in the prologue to his tale, vows to 'quyte' (better) the knight's tale. The narrator tries to dissuade the miller and goes on to apologize to the reader, claiming he is just repeating the miller's words as accurately as he can and that any readers who are likely to be offended should move on to another tale. The narrator also states that people should not 'maken earnest of game' or try to find any specific moral message in the miller's story. This last interjection from the narrator seems to deliberately foreground the contrast between the opening two tales. Whereas the knight's story is rich in the chivalric code, a clear moral imperative, the miller's story subverts any moral device, despite being rich in religious allusions.

By setting up such clear contrasts between the characters and the stories that they tell, Chaucer is able to present a series of snapshots of English life in the fourteenth century. The pilgrims' language and attitudes, humour and dialects are all explored and displayed. The different characters squabble amongst themselves and take issue and offence at each other's tales. 'The Reeve's Tale', a response from a pilgrim affronted by the miller, although also using the fabliau form, is much darker than the preceding tale. The narrator attempts to replicate a northern dialect in 'The Reeve's Tale' by changing the spelling of certain words, mostly by substituting the letter 'o' for the letter 'a' in words such as 'know' (knaw) and 'home' (hame) and using other, less familiar colloquialisms and vocabulary.

Some tales, usually those told by members of the group from the higher social strata, such as the knight or the nuns, employ lots of words borrowed from French and Latin, whereas 'The Miller's Tale' contains very few loan words. From time to time, characters such as the Wife of Bath or the Pardoner use the platform provided for them as a confessional, the former to describe her attitudes to love and marriage, the latter to reveal the corruption of the Church and the trade in bogus saints' relics.

Piece by piece, like a jigsaw puzzle, Chaucer constructs a vivid picture of medieval life in England. His pilgrims' appearance, manners, stories and personalities are all held up for scrutiny and described in a rich variety of linguistic forms from the rhyme royal of medieval poetry to plain prose littered with colloquialisms, jokes and obscenities.

Although Chaucer was certainly not the only author writing in the English of his day, *The Canterbury Tales* has ensured that he is the most famous. It is probable that its initial impact on language was small, as it may have been intended as a court entertainment only. However, its popularity endured and the first printed text of *The Canterbury Tales* was published in 1478.

—◦◦◦—

The Decline of French

By the latter half of the fourteenth century, the influence of French upon English society began to decline. There were a number of reasons for this, among them the fact that England was engaged in the Hundred Years War with France and the Black Death arrived, killing thirty per cent of the population of England and challenging the authority of government and the Church. Labour shortages led initially to higher wages, and when the government tried to quash these, there was deep resentment among the labouring classes, leading to the Peasants' Revolt of 1381.

> The poem *Piers Plowman*, attributed to William Langland and written between 1360 and 1387, is considered to be one of the great works of Middle English literature. At a time when the common people were suffering greatly, the poem seeks not to entertain the court but to give account of a true Christian life. The poem became linked to the Peasants' Revolt and may have been banned. William Caxton printed neither the Bible nor *Piers Plowman* – possibly for political reasons.

The Late Middle English period was a time of upheaval in England. Henry IV and Henry V recognized that if English people were to pull together, they needed to have a common language (many of the regional English dialects varied so greatly that travellers would struggle to understand and make themselves understood). One of the ways in which they approached this was to change the language of Parliament from French to English. So we enter a period where English kings spoke English and saw to it that English was taught in schools.

During the Wars of the Roses (1455–87), there was yet another period of social and linguistic change. As the social mix was shaken up, so language changed to accommodate this. Towards the end of the fifteenth century, English began to stabilize – the era of Modern English was on its way.

The lasting legacy of Norman French can be seen in the number of loan words that entered the English lexicon between the Conquest and the fourteenth century. It is estimated that around ten thousand words were incorporated into English during this period. Many of these words are related to officialdom, the law and administration: 'chancellor', 'exchequer', 'bailiff', 'summons', 'warrant', 'larceny', 'perjury', 'treason', 'libel', 'evidence', 'decree' etc. Other words are everyday nouns related to food and drink, house and home and clothing: 'fruit', 'mustard', 'salmon', 'herb', 'cloak', 'button', 'petticoat', 'wardrobe', 'closet', 'parlour', 'pantry' and 'ceiling'. Of the 10,000 words found in Middle English manuscripts, around seventy per cent are still in common usage in Modern English.

—◦◦◦—

Chancery Standard

The Court of Chancery in medieval England consisted initially of a collection of scribes assigned the job of documenting the official activities of the court. The scribes were an essential part of the royal entourage, following the monarch around, drawing up charters, laws and edicts and recording different facets of royal household business, rather in the manner of official secretaries or personal assistants to the monarch.

Only a small percentage of the English population at this time were literate. When people wanted something written down, they dictated to scribes.

The Chancery existed in this fragmented form prior to the Norman invasion, but became more formalized during the reign of William I. The Norman obsession with systematic record keeping as a requirement of effective and efficient government, eventually led to the creation of the Chancery Office in Westminster, London.

Until about 1400, everything was documented in French and Latin. However, during the reign of Henry IV and Henry V, written English began to be used for business matters, law and for literature. This was no easy task. The spread of different regional dialects across the country, each with their own pronunciation, led to considerable confusion when it came to spelling. For example, common words like 'such' and 'people' were spelt in various forms including 'sich', 'sych' and 'seche' and 'peeple', 'pepil' and 'peopull', depending in which part of the country the documents were produced.

A pressing need for standardization in the spelling of everyday words was apparent. This was particularly true of the Charter Roll, given that it concerned matters relating to the laws of the land. As a result, the scribes of Chancery set about creating a standard form of English for officialdom and many of the choices they made eventually became the accepted spelling in standard Modern English.

The dialects of Middle English are usually divided into four groups: Southern, East Midland, West Midland and Northern. After the 1430s, official records were mainly based on the East Midland dialect. It was this form of English that William Caxton adopted for his printing press in 1476.

——◦◦◦——

The Great Vowel Shift

Just as English was trying to get a little sorted, it encountered another challenge. One of the main conundrums in English language development is the stark difference between Middle English and Early Modern English. To contemporary sensibilities the language of Chaucer is difficult, the spelling archaic and foreign sounding. The language of Shakespeare on the other hand, is relatively easy to read and understand, with many words spelt or spoken much as they are today. It seems logical to assume that during the two hundred or so years between *The Canterbury Tales* and Shakespeare's early plays, English underwent a radical transformation in the form in which words were written and spoken.

This period of linguistic upheaval (roughly between 1350 and 1550) is referred to as the Great Vowel Shift. The term was first coined by Otto Jespersen, a Danish professor of linguistics at Copenhagen University at the turn of the twentieth century. Jespersen tracked changes in the pronunciation of English vowel sounds. Middle English contained seven long vowels (sounds elongated in speech) and, over time, these seven sounds condensed or 'shifted' into the form common in Early Modern English (with two long vowels becoming diphthongs). For example, the Middle English long vowel ʊ: (as in the word 'shoe' in Modern English) underwent a transformation to the sound əʊ (as in 'show') and eventually becoming the aʊ (as in 'shower'). As each long vowel shifted it set off a chain reaction with another vowel, forcing it to also shift while ensuring there was adequate space between the sounds to differentiate between them. For example, in Middle English, the word 'hate' would have been pronounced 'hart' and 'boat' pronounced 'boot'. This movement of vowel sounds probably affected different sections of the population at different times.

Scholars are in disagreement over which vowel shifted first to set the ball rolling. The dispute centres on what the noted English professor of linguistics David Crystal has termed the 'push me/pull you' axis. The pulling vowel shift theory states that the first vowel to move was i: (as in 'see') pulling the other long vowels upwards to the top of the mouth, the adjacent vowel ɛ moving into the space left by the preceding vowel was eventually to give

aɪ (as in 'dice'). The alternative view, the 'pushing' chain, contends that the first **aɪ** vowel (as in 'game') the first vowel to start the chain by moving upwards from the back and forcing the other long vowels forward. A third, more contemporary theory, combines the pushing/pulling argument by stating that as it seems likely that the shift occurred over time, to different dialects in different areas of the country, there could have been two or more smaller shifts as opposed to one uniform movement of speech sounds from the back and front of the mouth.

There are conflicting ideas as to the reasons behind the Great Vowel Shift. One theory is that the Black Death pandemic of the fourteenth century caused the population to move southwards towards London and southern England, causing lots of conflicting dialects to mix and merge together. Others blame the scribes of Chancery and their efforts to standardize English, or the later development of the printing press. Whatever the reason, the period of the Great Vowel Shift had a huge effect upon the way English developed into the language of the modern age, and although the condensing and movement of vowels appears to have continued up until the eighteenth century, the period between Chaucer and Shakespeare evidenced the most change.

PART FOUR

EARLY MODERN ENGLISH: A LEVIATHAN OF LANGUAGE

(1475 – 1670)

*'To write or even speak English is not a science
but an art. There are no reliable words.
Whoever writes English is involved in a
struggle that never lets up even for a sentence.
He is struggling against vagueness, against
obscurity, against the lure of the decorative
adjective, against the encroachment of Latin
and Greek, and, above all, against the worn-
out phrases and dead metaphors with which
the language is cluttered up.'*
GEORGE ORWELL, ENGLISH NOVELIST
(1903-50)

———

If the Middle English period was one of upheaval,
suppression and change, then it can be seen as paving
the way for the Renaissance period (the cultural and artistic
movement dating from the late fifteenth century to the
early seventeenth century) and the eruption of English.

The evolution of English through the Middle English
period continued, but the Elizabethan age saw radical
advances that laid the foundations for English as a global
language. New trade routes and world exploration,
combined with giant advances in science and technology,
were matched by an explosion of written language. The
introduction of William Caxton's printing press and mass
publishing coincided with this great flowering of art and
culture. The Early Modern era is sometimes referred

to as 'The Golden Age' of English literature, the age of Shakespeare, Bacon and Milton.

Rather like Thomas Hobbes's mythical sea monster, the English language in this epoch devoured words and ideas and began to stretch its tentacles out across the world.

—⎯⎯⟨∿∿⟩⎯⎯—

William Caxton and the Printing Press

William Caxton is often mistakenly credited with inventing the printing press. In truth, printing technology had been developing across parts of Europe for several centuries prior to Caxton setting up his printing company in 1476. Details of Caxton's early life are sketchy but it is thought he was born into a family of minor nobility around 1422.

Surviving records show he was apprenticed to a successful London merchant named Robert Large in 1438. Large was Master of The Worshipful Company of Mercers, an important organization that regulated and administered the livery trade, in particular the import and export of wool, silk and other fine fabrics.

Around 1450, Caxton settled in Bruges, a renowned centre for the European textile trade, and carved out a career as a successful businessman and diplomat. While in Bruges, Caxton became acquainted with Margaret of York, Duchess Consort of Burgundy, and as a master merchant he would have held some favour in the Burgundy court.

At some point, Caxton's business interests led him to travel across Europe and it is through this that he encountered the flatbed printing press. Germany had been at the forefront of developments in printing since the production of the Gutenberg Bible in 1455 and Caxton is known to have spent a period of time in Cologne acquainting himself with Johannes Gutenberg's revolutionary techniques.

Some accounts of Caxton's life give credit to Margaret of York for acting as patron and mentor to Caxton, and suggest that she encouraged him to return to England and introduce the new technology to the English language. Although undoubtedly a learned man, Caxton's primary skill was as a businessman and the commercial potential of the printing press was probably his main motivation.

In 1472, Caxton returned to Bruges and with the help of a local calligrapher, Colard Mansion, built a printing press. The first book Caxton's new press produced was a translation from French of Raoul Lefèvre's *Recueil des Histoires de Troye*, a popular French romance of the myths of the Trojan wars. Caxton translated the book and an early surviving addition has a frontispiece depicting Caxton presenting the book to Margaret of York as a gift, leading to the theory of her patronage as a key influence.

The book proved to be very popular with the Burgundy court and Caxton, sensing a shrewd commercial opportunity, returned to London and started a printing company in Westminster.

Between 1477 and his death in 1491, William Caxton is credited with printing around a hundred different texts in English. Caxton's books covered a wide range of subjects, from philosophy and classical romances, to poetry, prose and the works of Chaucer and Sir Thomas Malory. Many of the classical works Caxton translated himself and he provided interesting insights, in prefaces and epilogues, into the processes his books had been through.

Which Came First: 'Eggys' or 'Eryen'?

(see pages 86-7)

. . . to my hande came a lytyl booke in frenshe, whiche booke is named Eneydos made in latyn by that noble poete and grete clerke Vyrgyle.

And whan I had aduysed me in this sayd boke, I delybered and concluded to translate it in-to englysshe, And forthwyth toke a penne and ynke, and wrote a leefe or twyne whyche I ouersawe agayn to corecte it. And whan I sawe the fayr and straunge termes therin, I doubted that it sholde not please some gentylmen whiche late blamed me, syeing that in my translacyons I had ouer curyous termes whiche coude not be vnderstande of comyn people and desired me to vse olde and homely termes in my translacyons. And fayn wolde I satysfye euery man; and so to doo, toke an olde boke and redde therin and certaynly the englysshe was so rude and brood that I coude not wele understand it . . . And certaynly our langage now vsed varyeth ferre from whiche was vsed and spoken when I was borne . . . And that comyn englysshe that is spoken in one shyre varyeth from another.

WILLIAM CAXTON (C. 1422–91)

A merchant rather than a scholar, Caxton is often apologetic about some of his translations and seems to fret about the difficulties he has encountered.

Caxton understood that for his books to be commercially viable they needed to find an audience across the country. The proliferation of regional dialects, and the inconsistencies and anomalies in spelling and grammar, made for difficult decisions for the first publishers. However, despite these obstacles, the mass production of printed books made a major contribution to fixing written language into forms and rules. During the sixteenth and seventeenth centuries, some twenty thousand different books were published in the English language. A veritable explosion of printed material was read and circulated, and this precipitated the need to standardize written English in a manner which, in its various previous forms, it had always managed to resist.

In the prologue to his translation of Virgil's *Booke of Eneydos*, Caxton ruminates on the problems of translating into English at a time when the language was so fluid in terms of spelling, grammar and vocabulary. *Eneydos* was translated by Caxton from a French version of Virgil's epic *The Aeneid*, and Caxton illustrates his dilemmas and anxieties about his task with an anecdote which has become known as 'The Egg' story.

Two merchants who had been travelling abroad on business return to England and are sailing up the Thames when they run out of supplies. After anchoring their boat, they go ashore in search of food and happen upon a farmhouse. One of the merchants, named Sheffield, knocks on the door and requests of the farmer's wife the chance to buy some 'eggys'. The wife replies that she is very sorry but she doesn't speak French. This angers Sheffield as he doesn't speak French either. Eventually, the other merchant asks for some 'eryen' and the wife hands him some eggs. As Caxton writes, almost despairingly: 'Loo what sholde a man in thyse dayes now wryte, egges or eryen?' The problem occurred because Sheffield was using a Northern English dialect which was influenced by Old Norse, whereas his companion used the Southern Old English form 'eryen'. Caxton decides he is going to change the word again by spelling it 'egges'.

A high proportion of Caxton's publications were in English. It has been estimated that seventy per cent of the surviving texts from the fifteenth century were written in Latin and that Caxton printed about sixty-eight per cent of his editions in English, twenty-eight per cent in Latin, and four per cent in French.

Le Morte d'Arthur

The legends of King Arthur are an integral part of English folklore that have given rise to a whole genre of tales of swords and sorcery. The court of Camelot with its chivalrous Knights of the Round Table, Merlin the wizard and Excalibur, the sword in the stone (in some versions), are stories that have been told and retold in many different forms through the ages. The origins of these myths are unclear and stem from the oral story-telling tradition, but arguably they owe their enduring appeal to the endeavours of two men, Sir Thomas Malory and William Caxton.

Perhaps in keeping with the mysterious and magical aspects of his subject, very little is known for certain about Thomas Malory, with historians putting forward at least four possible people. The most common assumption is that he was a disgraced knight, who wrote while serving a prison term sometime between 1450 and 1470. Certainly research has thrown up some shady candidates. There is also dispute as to Malory's authorship of the work. The primary sources for the book are translations of classical French court romances dating from the thirteenth century onwards.

In this sense, Malory is taken to be more of a translator and compiler of different sources that he wove together into a coherent form and no doubt drew upon common English myths and added a few choice embellishments. Academic hair-splitting aside, the name Thomas Malory appears as the author on William Caxton's first printed edition published in 1485.

How Caxton came across the manuscript is also uncertain, or why he chose to publish it, but it is probable that, much as he had done with *Recueil des Histoires de Troye*, Caxton recognized the commercial potential in printing it. In *Le Morte d'Arthur* he had found a romance with quintessentially English appeal. The 1485 version proved to be something of a sensation and was reprinted several times during the sixteenth century, making it the first 'bestseller' in English fiction.

The influence of Caxton stems beyond that of merely a printer. Caxton, as was often his custom, rearranged and edited the different sections of the manuscript, wrote prefaces and afterwords to the different tales and changed the original title from the awkward and clunky *The hoole booke of kyng Arthur & of his noble knyghtes of the rounde table* to the more sophisticated Middle French, *Le Morte d'Arthur*.

In 1934, while undertaking a catalogue of the contents of the library of Winchester College public school, the Headmaster, W. F. Oakeshott, discovered a long-lost copy of *Le Morte d'Arthur*. After scholarly examination by a number of noted medieval scholars (among them the noted Russian-born Malory expert Eugene Vinaver), it came to light that Oakeshott had discovered a very early handwritten copy which had been marked up for type-setting, possibly by William Caxton. The 'Winchester Manuscript', as it is now known, proved to be a highly significant discovery as the text and organization of the book differed markedly from Caxton's printed version and thus showed how Caxton had diligently edited, corrected and re-ordered Malory's original.

Malory's original text was divided into eight books, beginning with the birth of Arthur and detailing his rise to prominence and the establishment of the Round Table. The separate books diverge to cover tales of other knights, such as Sir Gareth and Sir Lancelot, before returning to the stock Arthurian legends of the quest for the Holy Grail, the love affair between Queen Guinevere and Lancelot, and the betrayal and death of Arthur. Caxton subdivided Malory's eight books into twenty-one smaller books, grouping certain tales together thematically and splitting each book into chapters with summaries.

Le Morte d'Arthur is written in fairly blank and neutral prose, with little in the way of lavish description or linguistic innovation. Although Caxton published an edition of Chaucer's *Canterbury Tales* around the same time, the language of *Le Morte d'Arthur* is very different and contains none of Chaucer's poetic sensibilities and word play. In this respect it is something of an anomaly, with its matter-of-fact style more akin to the romances of Early Modern English than Middle English. The significance of Malory and Caxton's work lies in its huge popularity at the time and in cementing the enduring cult of the Arthurian legends.

By the mid-seventeenth century, *Le Morte d'Arthur* fell out of fashion, possibly on account of puritan objections to the ambiguous portrayal of the sin of adultery. The book was republished in 1816 and found a new readership during the Victorian era. Alfred, Lord Tennyson used Malory as the primary source for his cycle of twelve Arthurian verse poems *The Idylls of the King* (published between 1859 and 1885), and in 1892, the London publisher J. M. Dent commissioned Aubrey Beardsley to produce a lavishly illustrated deluxe edition of Caxton's text.

William Tyndale's Bible Translations

Language furnishes the best proof that a law accepted by a community is a thing that is tolerated and not a rule to which all freely consent.

FERDINAND DE SAUSSURE,
SWISS LINGUIST (1857–1913)

Reioyce and be glad for greate is youre rewarde in heven. For so persecuted they the prophets which were before youre dayes. Ye are the salt of the erthe.

TYNDALE'S TRANSLATION OF THE BIBLE

Although John Wycliffe and the Lollards were persecuted for trying to bring the word of God to the common people, many copies of Wycliffe's

Bible survived. This may have been that despite the book being banned and the severe penalties imposed for owning it, Wycliffe's Bible had an underground following supported by teams of subversive scribes who hand copied versions and distributed them in secret. As soon as the Church and state authorities seized a copy and burnt it, another one was being written out and passed around. It was inevitable then that, with new developments in printing in the late fifteenth century and the success on the Continent of the Gutenberg Bible (printed in the 1450s), that there would be a serious challenge to the ban on Bible translations.

The key figure in the fight to get the Bible translated into English was the Oxford-educated scholar and preacher, William Tyndale. Like Wycliffe before him, Tyndale believed that the Bible represented the true word of God and should not be censored and controlled, but available for all to read and study. In 1523, Tyndale travelled to London to try to secure permission to produce an English translation of the New Testament. The Church authorities were mindful of the influence on the Continent of the protestant reformer Martin Luther and the resulting large-scale civil unrest. They therefore flatly refused to sanction Tyndale's project. Undeterred, Tyndale fled to Germany, partly, as he quite rightly asserted, because he would find more sympathy for his ideas there, and partly to escape the attentions of the network of Catholic spies under the direction of Cardinal Wolsey, Henry VIII's proto chief of police.

During his exile in Germany, Tyndale worked on his

Bible. A richly-gifted scholar and multi-linguist, Tyndale chose to use the original Greek and Hebrew versions of the Bible as his sources, as opposed to the common Latin Vulgate which was endorsed by the Roman Catholic church. Tyndale was highly influenced by Erasmus, the Dutch theologian, and also by Martin Luther, both of whom Tyndale may have consorted with at this time.

Tyndale's Bible was printed in 1526 with an initial print run of six thousand copies. Plans were laid to smuggle the books into England. Cardinal Wolsey, however, was informed of the plans and instructed Henry VIII to deploy the Navy to patrol coastal waters and intercept and impound any boats found carrying Tyndale's translation. Although this Bible embargo met with some initial success, copies nonetheless found their way on to English shores, prompting the Church authorities to come up with a bizarre plan. A team of merchants travelled to the Continent and purchased all the remaining copies from the printer with the express intention of burning them in public.

Tyndale, albeit disgusted with the Church and its tyrannical powers, nonetheless saw a clear fallacy in their actions. Through the purchase of all the copies of his translation, he would receive a considerable sum of money – enough to clear his mounting debts and allow him to work on revisions and further translations. By attempting to crush him, the Church had inadvertently provided Tyndale with the means to continue.

Tyndale also predicted that the public burning of copies of the Holy Book would do little to impress the public and was more likely to help than hinder his cause.

Cardinal Wolsey condemned Tyndale as a heretic and a traitor and petitioned Holy Roman Emperor Charles V to extradite Tyndale to England. In 1530, Tyndale had written a public criticism of Henry VIII's divorce of Catherine of Aragon titled 'The Practyse of Prelates' and it was this as much as his Bible that enraged the king.

In 1535, Tyndale was arrested in Antwerp on charges of heresy and was tried and burned at the stake the following year. Tyndale's last words are reputed to have been, 'Oh Lord! Open the King of England's eyes'.

Tyndale's Bible, widely criticized at the time (Thomas More wrote that looking for errors in Tyndale's translations was akin to 'looking in the sea for water'), proved to be a big influence on future English Bibles.

Ironically, shortly after Tyndale's execution, Henry VIII commissioned an official English-language Bible (known as The Great Bible) which drew heavily on Tyndale's version and, despite the Archbishop of London, Richard Bancroft, directing the scholars of the King James Bible not to look to Tyndale for inspiration, this request seems to have been ignored and large portions of the Tyndale translation found their way into the King James version. The King James Bible is the most printed book in history and although there is no accurate record, the number of copies printed up to today is thought to be in billions. Tyndale may have died for his beliefs, but his voice lives on, not just in the Bible, but in our everyday speech.

Common Words and Phrases Attributed to Tyndale's Bible

William Tyndale is credited with introducing many new words and phrases to the English language through his Bible translations. Many of these words have specific religious connotations such as 'Passover' and 'Jehovah' and are derivatives of Hebrew terms; others are more commonplace such as 'fisherman', 'landlady' and 'broken-hearted'.

Tyndale's most telling influence is felt in introducing phrases that are used in everyday situations, often without the speaker being aware they are quoting the Bible. Below is a list of popular expressions attributed to William Tyndale:

Lead us not into temptation but deliver us from evil

Knock and it shall be opened unto you

Twinkling of an eye

A moment in time

Fashion not yourselves to the world

Seek and you shall find

Ask and it shall be given you

Judge not that you not be judged

The word of God which liveth and lasteth forever

Let there be light

The powers that be

My brother's keeper

The salt of the earth

A law unto themselves

Filthy lucre

It came to pass

Gave up the ghost

The signs of the times

The spirit is willing, but the flesh is weak

Punctuation, Pronouns and Standardized Spelling

As discussed previously, the establishment of the Chancery of Westminster in the 1430s set standard spellings for official state documents. In particular the use of 'I' in preference to 'ich' and a variety of other usages of the first person pronoun. The spelling of other words such as 'land' (the 'lond' of Chaucer) also became standardized in the modern form, alongside words like 'such', 'right', 'not', 'but', these, 'shall', 'should' and 'could'. The influence of Chancery Standard was keenly felt in the quest to develop Standard English. The East Midlands dialect had gained cultural dominance over the other dialects and flowed in through the political, commercial and cultural 'triangle' that joined London, Oxford and Cambridge.

However, the advent of the printing press and mass publication necessitated further developments in the standardization process. The Chancery clerks had adopted the East Midland variants and this naturally rubbed off on the London print houses. Some choices made by printers seem to have been quite arbitrary, however. For example, the adoption of the Northern dialect form 'they', 'their' and 'them' for plural and possessive pronouns, when the more common Southern dialect favoured 'hi', 'hir' and 'hem' (although this may have been simply to create a clear distinction with singular pronouns such as 'he', 'her' and 'him').

Caxton's anecdote about the eggs illustrates the task that typesetters had in finding a standard form that was easily comprehensible to all areas of the country. Furthermore, early proof-readers must have had a near impossible task, as books often contained multiple variations of spellings of the same word. Particular confusion centred on the use of double vowels and consonants; for example, 'booke' and 'boke' and 'fellow', 'felow' and 'felowe'.

One key difference between Early Modern English and Middle English can be seen in the use of double vowels and a silent final 'e' to indicate long vowels. Words such as 'name' were previously spelt 'nam' and 'soon' was spelt 'sonn'. Doubled consonants began to indicate short vowels in words such as 'getting' and 'netting'. In Middle English, spelling letters such as 'u' and 'v' and 'i' and 'j' were often transposable, but as the Early Modern era progressed, they evolved into vowels and consonants respectively.

Punctuation was another area in which usage and forms gradually became more standardized through printed language. Full stops became common at the end of sentences and the convention of using capital letters for proper nouns and at the beginning of sentences became commonplace.

The Fall and Rise of the Virgule

One casualty of punctuation reform was the virgule (an oblique stroke /). In Medieval manuscripts, the virgule was used to separate clauses in sentences and to join related items of information. This practice was widespread across most major European languages (the symbol itself was derived from ancient Roman script). However, during the Early Modern period the functions of the virgule were replaced by the comma.

> **Utopia:** Sir Thomas More was an important councillor to Henry VIII. In 1516, he published a book which, although written in Latin, gave us the word 'utopia'. The Utopia of More's book is an imaginary ideal island nation with an exemplary political system. Unfortunately, More's ideal was not to be. He strongly opposed Henry's break with the Catholic Church, was accused of treason and beheaded. Oddly, utopia in Greek means 'not a place' while eutopia means 'good place'.

After centuries of relative obscurity (though occasionally reappearing in place of the comma in various forms of experimental fiction during the mid-twentieth century), the virgule has experienced a renaissance in the digital age, where it is the standard form in the writing of hypertext transfer protocol (internet addresses).

Tottel's Miscellany

The Elizabethan age was marked by a flowering in poetry and song, through which many new forms and types of language were explored.

Songes and Sonettes, Written By the Ryght Honorable Lord Henry Howard, late Earle of Surrey, and other is the lengthy title for a work more commonly known as *Tottel's Miscellany*. The book, thought to be the first printed anthology of English poetry, was published in 1557, and provided a watershed moment in sixteenth-century literature. Many of the major Elizabethan writers at the start of the 'Golden Age, of English literature, including William Shakespeare, Christopher Marlowe and Edmund Spenser, were inspired by *Tottel's Miscellany*, particularly by the anthology's promotion of the sonnet form.

The collection was edited by the ground-breaking publisher Richard Tottel, who had a publishing firm at Temple Bar on Fleet Street. Tottel published many important translations of classic works, including the writings of Virgil and Boccaccio, but it is his seemingly modest collection of elegies, epigrams, sonnets, riddles, moral odes and love poetry for which he is revered. The principal poets in the collection were Henry Howard, Earl of Surrey, and Sir Thomas Wyatt. Howard, to whom the anthology is dedicated, was a prominent aristocrat at the court of Henry VIII and a close friend and associate of Wyatt. The inclusion of Howard and Wyatt's poems is significant because previously their work would have only been circulated for private consumption at Court and would not have found a wider audience.

Howard was cousin to two of Henry VIII's wives, Anne Boleyn and Catherine Howard, both of whom were beheaded, and himself holds the unfortunate distinction of being the last person to be executed by Henry VIII. The King, terminally ill and increasingly paranoid on account of acute syphilis, decided that Howard and his father, the Duke of Norfolk, were planning to usurp his son Edward after his death and ordered them both to be executed. Ironically, Thomas Howard, Henry's father, survived because the King himself died before the decree could be carried out.

Tottel's Miscellany contains 281 poems and epigrams, of which roughly half are attributed to Howard and Wyatt. Other prominent writers of the period such as Nicholas Grimand and John Heywood are also featured, as are ninety poems by anonymous authors. *Tottel's Miscellany* was published at the end of Mary I's reign, notorious for the purging of Protestant sympathizers, which is a possible reason for Richard Tottel withholding the authorship of some of the works.

One intriguing poem by Thomas Wyatt (along with another, 'Whoso List to Hunt') is thought by some scholars to describe an affair with Anne Boleyn prior to her marriage to Henry VIII:

They flee from me, that sometime did me seek,
With naked foot stalking within my chamber:

Once have I seen them gentle, tame, and meek,
That now are wild, and do not once remember,
That sometime they have put themselves in danger
To take bread at my hand; and now they range
Busily seeking in continual change.

The subtle intrigue within some of the poems suggests that they disguised subversive intentions or, if not, could be read as doing so. Other poems in Tottel's collection, however, appear to be mere whimsy, although some do contain unabashed erotic suggestion.

By the end of the sixteenth century anthologies of poetry had become popular and poems which had been for private or courtly enjoyment only, were now available for general readership. Shakespeare 'borrows' verses from the collection in *The Merry Wives of Windsor* and *Hamlet* and quite flagrantly plagiarizes verses from one anonymous poem, 'Against him that had slaundered a gentlewoman with him selfe', in his narrative poem *The Rape of Lucrece*.

Shakespearian Sonnets or Howardian Sonnets?

William Shakespeare is the acknowledged master of the poetic form referred to as the Elizabethan or Shakespearian sonnet. However, Shakespeare did not create the English sonnet form and although his name is often synonymous with it, this is largely down to the popularity of his verses.

The English sonnet form was created by the two principal poets of *Tottel's Miscellany*, Henry Howard and Sir Thomas Wyatt. Both poets were keen classicists and translators of Italian poetry, particularly of Virgil and Petrarch. Wyatt introduced the Petrachian sonnet to English but it is Howard who adapted the rhyme scheme. Classic Italian sonnets contain fourteen lines divided into an octave (first eight lines) and a sextet (last six lines). Howard's English sonnet kept the fourteen-line structure but divided this into three quatrains (four-line alternate rhymes) finished with a two-line couplet.

The Inkhorn Debate

The sudden flowering of the arts and sciences during the English Renaissance brought with it an explosion in the development of language. The Elizabethans developed a love of language itself and a craze for new words. This led to a fashion for 'inkhorn terms', or rather words with their roots in other languages, namely Latin and Greek and in some cases Italian, French and Hebrew. However, not all embraced this. A fear emerged that this influx of foreign words would swamp the 'purity' of English and a group of prominent courtiers and scholars formed The English Linguistic Purism Movement to counter it.

The term 'inkhorn' (the name of the animal horns used for storing ink for quills) is believed to have first been coined by Thomas Wilson, a prominent politician and scholar in the court of Elizabeth I. In his text *The Arte of Rhetorique* (1553) Wilson argues:

> Among all other lessons this should first be learned, that wee neuer affect any straunge ynkehorne termes, but to speake as is commonly receiued: neither seeking to be ouer fine, nor yet liuing ouer-carelesse vsing our speeche as most men doe, and ordering our wittes as the fewest haue done. Some seeke so far for outlandish English, that they forget altogether their mother's language.

The classical scholar Sir John Cheke, a man fluent in Latin and Greek and one of the most learned men of his day, was another to take up the cause of defending the Anglo-Saxon language: 'I am of this opinion that our own tung should be written cleane and pure, unmixt and unmangeled with borowing of other tunges.'

Cheke produced an edition of the gospel According

to St Matthew . . . translated from the Greek (1550) which was obsessive in its rejection of the Latin original, replacing words such as 'crucified' with 'crossed', 'prophet' with 'foresayer' and 'parable' with 'byword'.

Cheke's fate was not to be a happy one. The man who had been made professor of Greek at Cambridge by Henry VIII, as well as tutor to his son Edward, had no more power to quench the 'inkhorn' words than he had to fight the changes that came with the accession of Mary I, in 1553. Strongly Protestant, Cheke was imprisoned that year, but was released in 1554 and permitted to go abroad. He was rearrested in 1556 and imprisoned in the Tower of London. Forced to denounce his Protestant beliefs, he is said to have died of shame. Cheke is held to have written some of the best plain prose of his time, and noted for his phonetic spelling. However, it is for his classical translations that he is most respected.

Other writers such as Sir Thomas Elyot and George Pettie were in favour of borrowing words from other languages. Elyot compiled the first published Latin-English dictionary and believed that Latin was part of 'the necessary augmentation of our language'. George Pettie, a writer of romances, is believed to have travelled extensively abroad and to have developed a love of foreign tongues. *A Petite Pallace of Pettie His Pleasure* (1576) is littered with borrowed and anglicized words from other languages and written in a self-consciously overblown and high-brow style. Pettie argued that if all inkhorn terms were removed from the English language, it would eventually become impossible to describe anything adequately: 'for what word can be more plain than this word plain'.

Eventually, a compromise of sorts was made, with certain words (often those relating to science and medicine) being 'allowed' into the lexicon; words such as 'skeleton', 'thermometer', 'atmosphere' and 'system'. Other, often more colorful words, were popular only for a short time and fell into disuse or were replaced with different terms meaning the same thing. The words 'demit'(to turn someone away) for example, 'anacephalize' (to repeat an argument or point of view), 'deruncinate' (to weed something out) and 'eximious' (excellent).

The Campaign For Plain English?

The Inkhorn Debate was the first known language debate of its kind, and would certainly not be the last. Oddly, the educated gentlemen involved chose to ignore the fact that their beloved English had never been a pure language. What they might have learned from their debate, as many more would, is that, for better or worse, it is impossible to fix language.

English, however, the language so despised by the Normans, was now a language held in high esteem, and one for which Englishmen were still fighting.

Today, the Plain English Campaign, which was founded in 1979, is alive and kicking – fighting for communication in clear language and against 'gobbledygook, jargon and misleading doublespeak'.

—◦◦◦—

The Bard and the Renaissance Theatre

The influence of the works of William Shakespeare is beyond dispute. In terms of the written word, only the various translations of the Bible can be considered to have had such a profound and enduring effect upon the development of English. Shakespeare's plays have been translated, read, taught, performed and revered across the globe for centuries. No other writer has attracted such disciplined scholarship or provoked so much debate and interpretation. Shakespeare remains at the centre of the National Curriculum in schools in the United Kingdom and the United States. The great Russian poet Boris Pasternak spent half his lifetime working and reworking the Sonnets in translations into his mother tongue. Stage, film and television versions of Shakespeare's plays continue to be produced and enjoyed around the world; all a testament to the lasting appeal of the greatest writer in the English language.

However, although most people can name a

Shakespeare play and many have read or seen one performed, few can cogently explain why Shakespeare has remained the pre-eminent figure of English literature for four hundred years.

The beauty of Shakespearean language lies in its adoption of new forms of poetic and linguistic expression. Written English remained relatively fluid and unstructured in the mid-sixteenth century, outside the 'official' language of law and governance. The playwright Christopher Marlowe had begun to experiment with writing popular plays in blank verse, and his influence upon Shakespeare, who is believed to have been embarking upon a fledgling career as an actor at the time, is palpable in the evolution of his style. Blank verse is poetry written in a form known as iambic pentameter and/or to a decasyllable structure.

Decasyllable structures are lines of poetry or prose composed of words with a total number of (approximately) ten syllables and were common in Latin poetry. Marlowe was classically educated at Corpus Christi College, Cambridge, and saw the potential to adopt the decasyllable form to create powerful and evocative theatrical speech. The following example, often cited as evidence of Marlowe's alleged atheist tendencies, illustrates how complex ideas could be condensed and encapsulated using blank verse:

> I count religion but a childish toy,
> And hold there is no sin but ignorance.
>
> PROLOGUE, *THE JEW OF MALTA*

In classical Greek and Latin verse the rhythm of a line is determined by the weight of the syllables. A 'long syllable' in a word was one that literally took longer to pronounce. Typically, classical verse used hexametric structures comprising lines of six (hex) 'feet'. Each 'foot' being a pair or sequence of syllables (e.g. a long syllable followed by one or two short syllables). In English blank verse, the metric 'foot' is an unstressed syllable followed by a stressed syllable, as in the word 'explain' (ex-plain). These pairings of syllables are known as 'iambs', hence five iambs or feet to a line of ten syllables represents the classic iambic pentameter of Shakespeare's verse.

Shakespeare's early works were composed in blank verse, most notably *Titus Andronicus*, which uses the form liberally in dialogue between the characters. However, some scholars have noted that this sometimes leads to a flattening of the sense of individual character's speech or to a slowing down of the plot. As Shakespeare's style developed, he started to experiment with the iambic pentameter structure by subtly varying the length of sentences and occasionally inverting the unstressed/ stressed syllable groupings. The famous opening line from *Richard III* starts with the stress on the first word before reverting back to conventional iambs:

Now is the winter of our discontent ...

In the mature phase of his plays (1605–13), Shakespeare developed the iambic variations further to include extra unstressed or feminine endings to lines.

The most famous line of all, from *Hamlet*, contains this sudden switch in the rhythm, and so therefore, strictly speaking, it is not iambic pentameter at all, despite often being quoted as an example:

To be, or not to be: that is the question ...

This highly stylized and mannered method of writing speech was to provide actors with lines they could declaim to the audience, thereby drawing a distinction between the speech and the actions of the characters on the stage and the crowd watching from the stalls below.

The Elizabethan theatre was a hugely popular form of entertainment for the public, with the participation of the crowd often volatile and ribald in the extreme. In this sense, it seems incongruous that a largely illiterate population would be able to understand the language Shakespeare used, given its richness of metaphor and allusion, and unconventional speech rhythms. However, by popularizing stories from historical sources and creating engaging comedies, tragedies and romances, the Elizabethan theatre promoted the development of the English language.

Shakespeare was a prolific wordsmith. The *Oxford English Dictionary* cites over two thousand words found in Shakespeare's poetry and plays, which were not written down elsewhere prior to the late sixteenth century. Some words he coined for particular effect or to expand dramatic expression; others were borrowings from other languages. Many common phrases and idioms that we take for granted or even regard as clichés today can be traced back to Shakespeare's works.

Shakespeare Trek

Modern popular culture is littered with references and borrowings from Shakespeare's works, the most curious example being the science-fiction television and film franchise *Star Trek*. Early episodes of the original 1960s series made frequent references to Shakespeare's works, thinly disguising and reworking elements of the plots and characters from the plays into futuristic settings. The famous split infinitive during the opening sequence of the programme, 'To boldly go where no man has gone before' is written in slightly off-kilter iambic pentameter, reminiscent of Shakespeare's mature experiments with blank verse. This habit of liberally borrowing from Shakespeare progressed to naming whole episodes with Shakespeare quotes and regularly having the characters quote lines to each other.

The reasons for the *Star Trek* writers' obsession with Shakespeare are unclear, although one, possibly apocryphal explanation exists. The star of the original show, William Shatner (Captain James T. Kirk), was a classically trained actor who had a distinguished early career in Canadian repertory theatre before moving into television. It is thought that the writers of the original series were bemused at Shatner's notoriously haughty ego and, as a sly joke, began writing Kirk's lines in iambic pentameter and slipping in as many Shakespeare references as they could possibly get away with.

Common Phrases Derived from Shakespeare

Hundreds of the everyday words and phrases we use today are attributed to Shakespeare. Some of these are actually borrowings from other sources such as early medieval poetry or passages from the Bible, but they are known to us, because of his plays.

For example 'as white as driven snow' from *A Winter's Tale*' and 'a tower of strength' from *Richard III*, are lifted directly from the Old Testament. Conversely, 'in the twinkling of an eye', from *The Merchant of Venice* (First Quarto, 1600), appears in Corinthians in the King James Bible, which was not published until 1611.

Below are some well-known phrases, each derived from a different Shakespeare play.

A laughing stock (*The Merry Wives of Windsor*)

As dead as a doornail (*Henry VI*)

Eaten out of house and home (*Henry IV, Part 2*)

I will wear my heart upon my sleeve (*Othello*)

Laugh (yourselves) into stitches (*Twelfth Night*)

A pound of flesh (*The Merchant of Venice*)

Give the devil his due (*Henry IV*)

The better part of valour is discretion (*Henry IV*)

More in sorrow than in anger (*Hamlet*)

Too much of a good thing (*As You Like It*)

Vanish into thin air (*The Tempest*)

More sinned against than sinning (*King Lear*)

Milk of human kindness (*Macbeth*)

Parting is such sweet sorrow (*Romeo and Juliet*)

Something in the wind (*The Comedy of Errors*)

The more fool you (*The Taming of the Shrew*)

Spotless reputation (*Richard III*)

[To] play fast and loose (*Love's Labour's Lost*)

[To] make a virtue of necessity (*The Two Gentlemen of Verona*)

It was Greek to me (*Julius Caesar*)

'False Friends' and Faux Pas

A 'false friend' is a term used by linguists to describe words that appear to be similar or sound similar in two languages but have conflicting meanings, sometimes subtle in terms of context, often profoundly different in terms of usage. The word 'sensible' in Spanish is used to describe a person with a sensitive or compassionate disposition, not necessarily common sense. A native of Finland may receive strange looks in an English restaurant for ordering 'canine' stew (the Finnish word 'kaniini' means rabbit). 'Affluence' in France does not denote an abundance of personal wealth but a large, often spontaneous gathering of people.

There are many words in Modern English which, although similar in the Middle and Early Modern period, have seen their core meaning change in terms of everyday use. Such is the fluidity of the English language, that meanings change rapidly from generation to generation. Obvious examples of this can be found in slang and pejorative language uses, with the most contentious words often relating to minorities or marginalized groups in society. When Chaucer wrote in 'The Miller's Tale', 'And all above there lay a gay sautrie, On which he made a-nyghtes melodie So swetely that all the chambre rong'. It is clear that the word 'gay' is used to mean happy and bright. However, many other familiar words in Chaucer and Shakespeare present greater challenges to modern readers as the context in which a word was used has changed over time. Below is a list of five examples from

Shakespeare (there are countless more), where modern coinage differs markedly from its sixteenth-century equivalent.

naked

In modern usage naked means simply to be without clothes, but in the sixteenth century it had a variety of meanings. Hamlet writes to his Uncle Claudius that 'I am set naked on your kingdom' (*Hamlet*, IV.vii.) and by this he means not that he is forced to walk around nude, but that he has been stripped of his birthright and his place as rightful heir. Othello, once a brave and noble soldier, is briefly disarmed during the bloody climax of the play and, racked with guilt, resolves to take his own life. When Gratiano, who is keeping Othello prisoner, refuses to give him a weapon, he cries: 'Or naked as I am I will assault thee' (*Othello*, V.ii). In this sense, naked is taken to mean defenceless or disarmed.

gale

In meteorological terms a gale, especially at sea, is a cause for considerable concern but in Shakespeare's time 'a merry gale' or 'a happy gale' was synonymous with a fresh spring breeze and had none of the air of foreboding that a gale warning has today.

generous

The common meaning of generous is to share selflessly with others or to be unselfish in actions or words and therefore 'generous of spirit'. In Shakespeare's time, to be generous meant to be of noble and of aristocratic breeding. Hence, Desdemona's description of the court of Cyprus as 'generous islanders' (*Othello*, III. iii) does not suggest that the invitation to a banquet was anything other than a chance to meet with people of prestige and importance. The modern sense of the word generous may have developed later, with notions of charity being administered by the aristocracy towards the impoverished.

vicious

The word vicious as relating to physical and mental malice is a usage that developed in relation to the treatment of animals, particularly horses, during the eighteenth century. In Middle English however, a vicious person was somebody who was flawed in some way, or worthy of blame due to their inherent actions or faults. When Hamlet describes men as having 'some vicious mole of nature in them' (*Hamlet*, I.iv), he is ruminating on their emotional defects, not on a tendency towards violence.

sensible

'Before my God, I might not this believe, without the sensible and true avouch, Of mine own eyes' declares Horatio on first witnessing the ghost at the start of *Hamlet* (*Hamlet*, I.i). Interestingly, 'sensible' here has a meaning closer to the modern Spanish word than to the modern English usage, as Horatio is appealing to the evidence of his senses and the sensitivity of his perceptions and not to his common sense. (As a learned man, he had previously dismissed the rumours of a ghost haunting the battlements as 'fantasy'). Shakespeare did on occasion use 'sensible' in the modern sense of reliable and upstanding but more commonly used it to describe characters' sensitivity to feelings and emotions.

—◦◦◦—

Sir Francis Bacon

Sir Francis Bacon (1561–1626) was a leading philosopher, scientific writer, lawyer and politician during the reigns of Queen Elizabeth I and James I. Bacon's work covers a wide range of subjects encompassing natural philosophy, contemporary politics, law, scientific methodology and questions of ethics.

Bacon was born into a wealthy aristocratic family; his father, Sir Nicholas Bacon, was Lord Keeper of the Great Seal and his grandfather was Sir Antony Cooke, a noted humanist and tutor to Edward VI. Bacon's early education was conducted at home under the tutelage of John Walsall. At the age of twelve, Bacon entered Cambridge University where he was taught by Doctor John Whitgift, a controversial clergyman who later became Archbishop of Canterbury.

Bacon was a richly gifted student with an enquiring mind and, while at Cambridge, was introduced to Queen Elizabeth I. On completion of his studies, Bacon was appointed as a diplomatic aide to the English ambassador in Paris and travelled extensively around Europe studying languages and law.

After the death of his father, Bacon returned to take up a position at Grey's Inn. However, failure to gain high office in law led him to turn his attention to politics and enter the Houses of Parliament. Bacon sat in both houses at various times during his life, as an MP in the House of Commons and as a life peer. He served James I as Attorney General and Lord Chancellor. Despite achieving his ambitions of attaining high office, Bacon's political career was chequered and ended in disgrace when he was charged with corruption for accepting bribes. Bacon pleaded with Parliament for clemency, admitting to accepting gifts, but claiming such favours had not coloured his judgement. Parliament barred Bacon from any future office in politics and briefly imprisoned him in the Tower of London.

There is considerable speculation as to the extent to which Bacon was embroiled in corrupt activities while serving as Lord Chancellor. Bacon's closeness to the throne as counsel to King James is thought to have made him many powerful enemies. Accepting gifts and handouts from interested parties was common practice in the parliament of the day and Bacon's admission of guilt may have been due to him being blackmailed over allegations of homosexuality.

Deprived of his power and influence, Bacon retreated to his studies and devoted the remainder of his life to writing and conducting scientific experiments. He died in 1626 from pneumonia, which some historical accounts claim he contracted while testing the possibility of preserving meat by freezing it in compacted snow.

Did Francis Bacon Write Shakespeare's Plays?

Since the mid-nineteenth century, various writers and scholars have proposed the theory that Shakespeare's plays were written by Sir Francis Bacon using 'Shakespeare' as a pseudonym, or that they were written by a team of writers of which Bacon was the leader. This questioning of Shakespeare's authorship seems to rest upon the scant information available about his personal life, the range of genres his opus encompasses and the differences in style and tone between certain plays.

Despite the best efforts of amateur sleuths and conspiracy theorists, who have based their arguments largely around spurious cryptograms they claim to have discovered and unravelled, cunningly concealed within Shakespeare's plays, there is no evidence at all that Bacon had anything to do with writing for the theatre.

Alongside his political and legal activities, Bacon's scientific and philosophical output was prodigious. It would have been virtually impossible for Bacon to have had the time to write and produce over thirty stage plays and one hundred and fifty sonnets. This, however, has not stopped over two hundred books being written on the subject and the formation of the Francis Bacon Society which is devoted to promoting the theory.

The First Poet Laureate?

When James VI of Scotland and I of England came to the throne in 1603, many were quick to court his favour. Among these was the playwright Ben Jonson. In spite of often being in trouble with the authorities, and managing to be present at a dinner attended by the conspirators of the Gunpowder Plot of 1605, Jonson held on to the King's goodwill. In 1616, he received a yearly pension of about £60, leading some to call him England's first Poet Laureate.

The King James Bible

The King James Bible is often described as the most important book in the English language and the one single source that has had the deepest influence on the way English has evolved over the last four hundred years. Common idiomatic phrases such as 'salt of the earth' or '(to put) words in to one's mouth' are attributed to the King James Bible which, due largely to the Pilgrim Fathers, who made it required reading, remains the most widely read version of the Bible in the United States.

The influence of the translation had a huge impact on the spread of English throughout the British Empire due to its popularity during the Victorian era, a testament to its power and authority. However, when it was first published in 1611, its subsequent enduring appeal would have been difficult to predict.

In 1604, James I convened a conference of senior Church of England clerics at Hampton Court. The principle reason for the meeting was to try to repair the simmering factions within the Church caused by the rise of the Puritan movement during the Reformation. The Puritans objected to elements of the previously printed English Bibles and lobbied the King to sanction a state-authorized version. Chief among the Puritan campaigners was the cleric and scholar John Reynolds, who believed a single official version to be read in church would help cement the unity of service and personalized worship that the Puritan movement upheld.

King James agreed, partly as a concession and attempt to dispel Puritan discontent and partly due to personal issues with the Geneva Bible, which was the prominent translation used in churches at the time. The Geneva Bible contained some marginal notes that James believed criticized the divine right of the royal throne, and it referred to certain kings in the Old Testament as 'tyrants'.

The new translation was undertaken by a team of scholars drawn from the Universities of Oxford, Cambridge and Westminster. The teams were divided into six committees (two based in each centre) with eight members, each with a designated supervisor. In all, fifty-four men, all but one ordained clerics of the Church of England, were initially employed to undertake the task (although only forty-seven remained on completion of the task) and they were paid a salary of twenty pounds a year for their labours.

The Archbishop of London, Richard Bancroft, set down a series of strict rules for the translation, the main stipulation being that, as far as possible, the new text should use as its model the Bishops' Bible of 1568.

As noted scholars well versed in Hebrew, Latin and Greek, the clerics set about producing individual translations which were then discussed within their separate groups before circulating their texts to the other five committees for further amendment and clarification. In 1610, the clerics met at Stationers Hall in London and spent the next year compiling the different translations into a consistent and coherent final text for printing. In 1611, the new translation was printed by Robert Barker, whose father had been made Royal Printer under Elizabeth I, thereby further adding the stamp of royal approval.

The King James Bible was an astonishing achievement of scholarship and organization. If the intention was to produce a standardized version to be used in all churches and services and thereby appease Puritan conventions, in reality it gave a unity of form and expression to the language of religion and faith. Many critics have pointed to the deliberate 'musicality' of the verses, which ebb and flow with an internal rhythm. This musical sense for the language chosen was partly a result of the scholars

The Bishops' Bible

After his break with the Catholic Church, Henry VIII had been keen to enforce Protestantism and sanctioned the translation of the Bible into English so that it could be read to the people – the very act that had previously invited a death sentence for all who attempted it. Thus came the Great Bible of 1539 – the first authorized edition of the Bible in English. Ironically, it drew heavily on Tyndale's Bible. However, when the Geneva Bible was published in Switzerland in 1560, by Protestant scholars who had fled from England during Mary I's reign, it was preferred by many readers. This angered the Church and, in 1561, Matthew Parker, Archbishop of Canterbury, commissioned a team of bishops to compile a new bible that would stand up to the Geneva one. The Bishops' Bible was first printed in 1568 and all clergy were ordered to own a copy. However, the Geneva Bible remained popular and is thought to have been used by William Shakespeare, Oliver Cromwell, John Milton, John Donne and John Bunyan.

reading passages aloud to test words for their appropriateness. The Bible was intended to be read in church services and so needed to have a consistency of voice and simplicity of vocabulary so that all of the congregation could understand its meaning.

In the preface written by Miles Smith, the Bishop of

Gloucester, the problems of translating from multiple sources and languages are addressed. The translators desired to avoid the repetitions common in the Latinate Bibles by substituting plain English words and phrasal variations, while avoiding the idiomatic language of the time. In terms of grammar, and given that the English language was undergoing far-reaching changes throughout the sixteenth and seventeenth centuries, the translators reverted to more archaic forms.

For example, although the singular 'you' was in common usage, the translators use 'thou' and 'thee' interchangeably throughout as both singular and plural. The overall effect is to render the Bible into a highly readable and accessible form, while retaining its sense of authority and linguistic resonance and power. In this respect, the scholars' seven years of painstaking study was the culmination of all the previous translators' work, cultured and refined for the common ear. As Bishop Smith humbly acknowledges in his preface, when he writes of previous translators: '[they] deserve to be had of us and of posteritie in everlasting remembrance, that whatsoever is sound alreadie, the same will shine as gold more brightly, being rubbed and polished.'

King James spoke fluent Greek, Latin, French, English and Scots and was also taught Italian and Spanish, so he should have had little trouble with the language of the English court. However, many remarked on his unkingly language. He supposedly had a vulgar sense of humour and once shouted at his Presbyterian ministers, 'I give not a turd for your preaching.' James had taken a keen interest in the poetry of his native tongue, but as his inheritance of the English throne grew nearer, his poets began to anglicize their writing. On a physical note, James also had the misfortune to suffer from an overlarge tongue.

Who Owns the Copyright in the Bible?

Despite having the royal seal of approval, the King James Bible was not an immediate success and it took until the middle of the seventeenth century to fully supplant the Bishops' Bible as the official Bible used in church. This proved to be problematic to the Bible's printer, Robert Barker, who had invested considerable funds into printing the first version in 1611. Barker ran into crippling debt and was forced to farm out the printing of certain portions of the text to two other printers, Bonham Norton and John Bill.

Although born of necessity, Barker's arrangement with his rival printers proved to be disastrous. Bitter disputes arose over the sharing of the meagre profits and who owned the rights to print the different sections of the text. Years of legal actions followed, with, at one time, both printers producing rival additions or shortened versions. Eventually, in 1629, tired of the perpetual squabbling amongst London's printing fraternity, the Universities of Oxford and Cambridge gained permission from the Crown to produce revised editions of the text under the guidance of members of the original translation team.

'No Man Is An Island'

In 1615, Catholic-born John Donne (1572–1631) became an Anglican priest, on the orders of King James VI and I, and went on to become Dean of St Paul's Cathedral. Donne led a colourful life, including a secret marriage that landed him in the Fleet Prison for a short time and a long stretch of poverty thereafter, having several children to support. Donne was also an influential satirist and poet, thought to be the greatest of the Metaphysical Poets, which included George Herbert, Richard Crashaw, Andrew Marvell and Henry Vaughan. Some of his lines have entered common parlance, as this, from the passage in one of his sermons that begins 'No man is an island, entire of it self': 'And therefore never send to know for whom the bell tolls; it tolls for thee.'

Various revised editions, official and pirated, sprung up over the next hundred years, until Cambridge University published a revised edition in 1760, which provided the basis for the 1769 standard text under the editorship of Benjamin Blayney. This edition has remained more or less unchanged to this day.

In the strictest terms, the monarch, as head of the Church of England, owns the copyright of all versions of the Anglican Bible. In practice, this is not enforced, and all significant translations are in the public domain – a testament to men such as Wycliffe and Tyndale who devoted their lives to giving ownership of the Bible back to the people.

—————

Thomas Hobbes's *Leviathan*

Thomas Hobbes (1588–1679) was the pre-eminent English philosopher of the seventeenth century, whose most influential work, *Leviathan*, provided the basis for social contract theory, the starting point of western political philosophy. *Leviathan* was written during a period of wholesale political and social upheaval on account of the English Civil War. Hobbes, a royalist who believed in the absolute power of the sovereign through consensus of the subjects, was understandably fearful of the consequences of civil war. Indeed, fear of a society that turns upon itself is one of the central totems of *Leviathan*.

Very little is known of Hobbes's early life. In his biographical writings, Hobbes claimed he was born prematurely on the eve the Spanish Armada approached the English coast. He believed the terror his mother felt caused her to give birth through shock. He wrote: 'fear and I were born as twins together'. After attending a small private school in Malmesbury, Wiltshire, Hobbes entered Magdalen College, Oxford at the age of sixteen. He does not appear to have been a particularly diligent student, taking six years to gain his Bachelor of Arts degree, but on leaving university he took up a post as a private tutor to the children of William Cavendish, Duke of Devonshire.

Hobbes's association with the Cavendish family proved to be fruitful in terms of his intellectual development. Hobbes travelled to the Continent with the duke's son William and this provided him with access to new scientific and philosophical methods and models. Hobbes began to develop a theory of motion and momentum through studying physical and natural phenomena. This led him to attempt to extend his system into the realm of political science in his 'The Elements of Law, Natural and Politic'. By applying notions of the natural order of things, Hobbes asserted that man in nature was essentially 'brutish' and driven by self-interest and his own needs. As he later wrote in Leviathan: 'The life of man is solitary, poor, nasty, brutish and short'.

Hobbes fled England on the eve of the Civil War in 1640 and settled in Paris, where he continued his scientific and philosophical inquiries. He was a member of an esteemed Parisian circle of prominent intellectuals, led by the theologian and mathematician Marin Mersenne and including Descartes and Pascal. During eleven years of exile, Hobbes worked as a private tutor to the deposed Prince of Wales (Charles II) and drafted his two principal works *De Cive* ('of the citizen') exploring his theory of the origins of civil society, and *Leviathan*.

Leviathan is divided into four parts. The first, 'Of Man', outlines Hobbes's philosophical framework, namely the state of man in nature and the causes of conflict and civil unrest that arise from this state. The second section explores different aspects of 'Commonwealth' or governance, with Hobbes concluding that 'monarchy' or the absolute rule of one representative over the masses is the most effective. In the final two sections, Hobbes turns his attention to religion, providing a critique of what he considered to be the misappropriation of aspects of the scriptures and drawing a distinction between the 'darkness of ignorance' and 'the light of true knowledge'.

In summary, *Leviathan* proposes that although all men are equal in nature there is a need for a social contract to bind society together and avoid the turmoil of discord and war. As such, if by consensus, society chooses to be ruled by the divine will of a monarch, they surrender part of their natural liberty in the interests of peace and protection from civil strife. Conversely, it is the duty of the monarch to ensure the protection of his subjects.

Thomas Hobbes: Twisted Fire-Starter?

In 1666, Oxford University ordered the wholesale burning of all copies of Hobbes's work on account of its rejection of traditional scholarly method, and amid Church accusations of heresy. Such was the backlash against Hobbes, questions were asked in Parliament during the inquest into the Great Fire of London (2–5 September 1666); it was suggested that the burning of Hobbes's books may have been a contributory cause of the blaze. Hobbes was known by his detractors as 'The Monster of Malmesbury'; they ridiculed his analogy of civil society as a 'leviathan' – an all consuming sea-beast from mythology – and called him 'The Bug-Bear of the Nation'.

Published on Hobbes's return to England in 1651, *Leviathan* proved to be highly controversial. Hobbes had hoped that his work would help to reform philosophical enquiry and stabilize England during a period of extreme upheaval and ultimately save civil society from 'the war of all against all'. Hobbes soon found himself under attack from all sides. The Parliamentarians rejected his support for the right of the monarchy to rule; staunch royalists were offended by his dismissal of the monarch being appointed by God and the Church, and accused Hobbes of atheism on account of his criticism of religious interpretation and scientific rejection of disembodied souls and spirits.

Although *Leviathan* found few admirers during Hobbes's lifetime, it is nonetheless regarded as one of the most important contributions to the development of political science. Hobbes's introduction of the theory of the social contract greatly influenced future writers such as his contemporary John Locke and Jean-Jacques Rousseau.

━━∍ひひ∾━━

John Milton and *Paradise Lost*

The Measure is *English* Heroic Verse without Rime, as that of *Homer* in Greek, and *Virgil* in Latin; Rhime being no necessary Adjunct or true Ornament of Poem or good Verse, in longer Works especially, but the Invention of a barbarous age, to set off wretched matter and lame Meeter; grac't indeed since by the use of some famous modern Poets, carried away by Custom, but much to thir own vexation, hindrance, and constraint to express many things otherwise, and for the most part worse then else they would have exprest them.

PREFACE TO PARADISE LOST, BOOK I

It is a well-worn cliché, yet the most notable literary figures to write in English in the Early Modern period adhere to the old joke about London buses. The language had waited (with a few minor exceptions) for a genius since Chaucer, two centuries previously, and suddenly half a dozen turned up almost at once. The century between the late 1580s and 1670s saw an explosion of brilliance in English literature: William Shakespeare, Ben Jonson, Christopher Marlowe, Francis Bacon, John Dryden and, considered by some the greatest of all, John Milton.

John Milton (1608–74) was a poet, scholar, philosopher and statesmen, best known for his epic poem *Paradise Lost*. The poem, composed in twelve books and running to over 10,000 lines of blank verse, is considered to be one of the masterpieces of literature in the English language. The poem recounts the casting out of Satan from Heaven and Satan's revenge through the temptation of Adam and Eve in the Garden of Eden, resulting in the fall of man and the creation of evil and sin.

Milton composed the poem over a five-year period between 1658 and 1663. At the time, Milton, who had served as a minister in Oliver Cromwell's Commonwealth Republic, was living in poverty and his reputation was tarnished by the restoration of the monarchy in 1660. The poem represents a remarkable feat of the imagination, both in scope and scale, particularly because Milton had gone almost completely blind due to chronic glaucoma.

Milton composed his poem by dictating lines to his amanuenses (scribes); mostly family and friends – his daughters and the poet Andrew Marvell. Earlier in his career, Milton had gained a reputation for being a free spirit and radical thinker. Educated at Christ's College,

Cambridge, where he displayed a particular aptitude for languages and the classics, Milton gained a Masters degree and then embarked upon an extensive period of self-education. A voracious reader, he consumed books on a wide range of subjects, from history and science to literature, philosophy and political theory.

Milton continued his interest in languages and is thought to have been adept in seven different tongues: Latin, Greek, Spanish, Italian, Hebrew, Dutch and Old English/Anglo-Saxon. In 1638, Milton embarked on a 'Grand Tour' of European centres of culture and learning. During his time in Italy, he ingratiated himself with prominent members of the local intelligentsia in Florence, Rome and Venice (he was introduced to, among others, the astronomer Galileo). This period of travel had a profound effect upon Milton, who developed an interest in Republicanism that was to shape his future career.

When Milton returned to England he found the country in turmoil and on the brink of civil war. Milton set about writing political tracts and radical pamphlets on a variety of subjects, from educational reform to withering attacks on Church corruption and the monarchy. Milton's support for Oliver Cromwell's Puritan and Republican movement led him to being appointed as Minister for Foreign Tongues under the Commonwealth Protectorate. Although this civil position largely involved translating and composing official parliamentary business into different languages, when correspondence was needed with other

Continental powers, Milton used the public platform for unofficial propaganda for the parliamentary cause.

Following Cromwell's death and the break-up of the Protectorate, Milton, who had made many enemies, was forced into a period of obscurity. It is during this time that he wrote *Paradise Lost*.

The poem is written in a highly-stylized form of blank verse which has become known as Miltonic verse. Milton was not the first to write in blank verse but adapted the form in innovative ways, which subsequently influenced later writers such as Alexander Pope, John Keats and William Blake.

Milton's blank verse is characterized by a unique and peculiar form of diction and use of vocabulary and grammar. For example: 'May serve to better us and worse our foes' uses the adjective 'worse' as a verb, while descriptions such as 'the vast of heaven' uses an adjective as a noun.

Milton also peppered his poetry with old-fashioned medieval words and expressions more akin to Old and Middle English, such as 'erst', 'grunsel', 'welkin', and 'frore', and was unapologetic that he deliberately eschewed any traditional rhyme scheme. Milton defends his abandonment of rhyme in the preface to *Paradise Lost* by likening it to a freedom of spirit that had been denied to his predecessors; an 'ancient liberty':

'This neglect then of Rhime . . . is to be esteem'd an example set, the first in English, of ancient liberty recover'd to heroic Poem from the troublesom and modern bondage of Rimeing.'

John Milton: King of the Metal Heads

Although undoubtedly a huge influence on the Romantic movement, and particularly the work of poets such as Percy Bysshe Shelley and William Blake, one area of popular culture where Milton's work has found a surprising resonance is with purveyors of heavy rock music. Over a dozen different heavy-metal bands from various parts of the world have written songs inspired by *Paradise Lost*, including the British band, Cradle of Filth, whose concept album, *Damnation and a Day* is inspired by Milton's epic poem.

PART FIVE

LATE
MODERN
ENGLISH:
TOWARDS
A GLOBAL
LANGUAGE

(1670 – 1900)

'If you describe things as better than they are,
you are thought a romantic; if you describe things as
worse than they are, you are thought a realist; if you
describe things as exactly as they are, then you are
thought a satirist.' QUENTIN CRISP,
ENGLISH WRITER AND RACONTEUR (1908–99)

—◦◦◦—

And was Jerusalem builded here,
Among these dark Satanic mills?
WILLIAM BLAKE, ENGLISH POET AND ARTIST (1757–1827)

The late seventeenth century brought with it a demand for order in language. The poet John Dryden (1631–1700) protested: 'We . . . have not so much as a tolerable dictionary, or a grammar, so that our language is in a manner barbarous'. In their frustration, scholarly English speakers turned once again to their knowledge of Latin. Dryden is said to have translated his thoughts into Latin so that he could express them perfectly in English.

The learned members of the Royal Society (founded in 1660) objected to anything that was unscientific in language. They wanted English to be plain rather than poetic: clear, precise, mathematical. While some did their best to harness, others continued to push boundaries, and trade continued to be an influence on English. The language of ships and shipping entered the general vocabulary, and

English absorbed foreign words from across the seas and the American colonies.

While many words were imported into the language, many more were exported. The Late Modern English period is characterized by the growth of English as a world language; the Industrial Revolution and the expansion of the British Empire being driving forces in the global spread of English between the eighteenth and twentieth centuries.

Printed material was now abundant, and more people could read, including women. Four times as many books were published by the end of the eighteenth century than at its beginning. In the early eighteenth century, there were twelve London newspapers and twenty-four regional papers. By the nineteenth century there were fifty-two London papers and over a hundred others. Additionally, cheaper printing allowed for a wider variety of publications.

Literacy figures of the eighteenth and nineteenth centuries are hard to gauge. It has been cited that literacy may have been as low as 30 per cent in the early eighteenth century and that, by the 1840s, as many as 70 per cent of people may have had some knowledge of reading and writing. Education for all was yet to be embraced, however. The upper classes saw it as dangerous; the working classes had little time or need to devote to it.

The rise of industrialism and the drive towards town living witnessed enormous social change. While conditions in factories were harsh, for the first time ordinary people had the chance to better themselves through higher wages, industrial opportunity and trade. In spite of poor living conditions and outbreaks of disease, the population rose dramatically. That of England more than doubled between 1801 and 1850 and nearly doubled again by the end of the century. People were also living longer.

This meant that there were suddenly millions more people speaking English. The rise of a new educated middle class, and the Victorians' moral drive to improve the lot of the poor (including schooling), also increased the number of literate English speakers.

The literature of the time enjoyed huge productivity and innovation in both poetry and prose. The eighteenth century saw the rise of the novel as a literary genre and the nineteenth-century novelists added to the canon of great English writers who are still read worldwide.

Alexander Pope

When those fair Suns shall sett, as sett they must,
And all those Tresses shall be laid in Dust;
This Lock, the Muse shall consecrate to Fame,
And mid'st the Stars inscribe Belinda's Name!

The Rape of the Lock

The poet and critic Alexander Pope (1688–1744) was a key figure in eighteenth-century literature and a major influence on English satire. Born into a Catholic family, Pope's formal education was severely disrupted by the Test Acts (1673–78) which, amongst other civil restrictions, effectively outlawed Catholic schools and barred Catholics from attending university. As a child, Pope was afflicted with constant health problems. He contracted Pott's disease, a virulent form of tuberculosis that causes curvature of the spine. Stymied by illness and the anti-Catholic dogma of the age, Pope set about educating himself by voraciously reading everything from epic poets such as Homer and Virgil to titans of English literature such as Chaucer, Shakespeare and Dryden. In addition to classical works, Pope also taught himself several languages so that he could read prominent writers in French, Italian and Greek.

After five years of painstaking study, Pope's precocious intellect attracted the attentions of a prominent London literary circle headed by the playwrights William Wycherley and William Congreve (a close friend of the great Irish satirist Jonathan Swift). They encouraged Pope in his career and helped him to publish his first major work, *Pastorals,* in 1709.

Pope's rise to prominence was heralded by the publication in 1711 of 'An Essay On Criticism', an ambitious attempt to analyse and discuss the 'rules' of poetry in poetic form. Pope took as his model the Roman satirical poet Horace, who had established the poem as essay form with his 'Ars Poetica'. 'On Criticism' is composed in heroic couplets of immaculate metre and revealed Pope, at the tender age of twenty-three, to be a gifted writer. The poem brought Pope instant fame and enabled him to firmly establish himself on the London literary scene.

Pope's masterpiece *The Rape of The Lock* (1712, revised 1714) further developed his use of classical forms by transposing Homer's epic poem form into a satirical attack on the pettiness and vanities of upper-class society. The poem is based upon a real incident in which Lord Petre is alleged to have inappropriately snipped off a lock of Lady Arabella Fermor's hair. Pope's intention was to try to broker a truce by holding up the subsequent 'feud' for gentle ridicule. *The Rape of The Lock* represents one of the finest examples (along with *Paradise Lost*) of epic poetry, or in this case mock heroic poetry, in the English language. Abundant with references to classical yore and with judicious details of the paraphernalia and decadence of his own time, Pope virtually redefined the possibilities of poetry and the language of satire.

After the success of *The Rape of The Lock*, Pope set about translating and annotating Homer's *Iliad* and *Odyssey* into English, and the money he received for his efforts provided him with much needed financial security. Pope was also a member of the satirists' circle 'The Scriblerus Club' – a loose collective of writers (including Jonathan Swift) who rallied against false scholarship and pedantry by writing hoax articles under the pen-name of a highly pompous, invented critic, Martinus Scriblerus.

Inevitably Pope's meteoric rise to fame and fortune attracted the petty jealousies of his contemporaries and his career went into sharp decline after a series of very public spats with other writers, publishers and critics. To some extent Pope was partly responsible for the stains on his reputation. The satire *The Dunciad*, a savage, thinly veiled attack on his growing army of critics and detractors, was a commercial success, but the ensuing scandal opened old wounds with Pope's enemies and added a fair few more to the queue. The poem is written in Pope's signature mock-heroic form and concerns a mythical kingdom called Dulness, populated by idiots and dunces and people of questionable taste. By virtually naming his targets in person and satirizing their habits and opinions, Pope was unlikely to win any popularity contests.

Alexander Pope is the third most cited English writer in the *Oxford English Dictionary of Quotations*, after Shakespeare and Milton. Pope brought classical technique, poise and virulent satire to English poetry for the first time properly since Chaucer.

Samuel Johnson's *Dictionary of the English Language*

Language is a process of free creation; its laws and principles are fixed, but the manner in which the principles of generation are used is free and infinitely varied. Even the interpretation and use of words involves a process of free creation.
NOAM CHOMSKY, AMERICAN LINGUIST, PHILOSOPHER AND HISTORIAN (B.1928)

Samuel Johnson's *A Dictionary of the English Language* was published in 1755 to great critical acclaim and remained the primary authority on the English lexicon until the creation of the *Oxford English Dictionary* in the later half of the nineteenth century. There had been several previous attempts to compile English dictionaries, the first known dated in the early sixteenth century.

The expansion in publishing and the technology of printing in the eighteenth century, combined with a dramatic rise in literacy, necessitated a need for a definitive dictionary to be produced. As a consequence, several London publishers, including Thomas Longman of Longmans fame, came together to jointly fund a wide-arching review of the language. Johnson was chosen as the principal scholar and compiler and was paid £1,500 to complete the project.

The publishing consortium most likely assumed that Johnson would sub-contract some of the work to other scholars or employ a team of researchers. Amazingly,

Johnson (apart from minor clerical assistance) undertook the project completely on his own, making his dictionary perhaps the greatest work of scholarship ever undertaken by a single person in English.

Samuel Johnson (1709–84) was born in Lichfield and briefly attended Oxford University before being forced to abandon his studies due to financial hardship. Prior to the publication of the dictionary project, Johnson had been building a reputation in literary circles as an essayist, biographer, journalist and literary critic and wrote regularly for several prominent, fashionable London journals and periodicals. In addition to his non-fiction writing, Johnson was also a poet and dramatist of some renown and an important figure on the London literary scene.

Johnson began preparing the groundwork for his dictionary in 1746 by producing a 'plan' that outlined his methodology. In Johnson's opinion, previous dictionaries resembled lists of words with little explanation of the context in which they were used. In his preface, Johnson wrote: 'wherever I turned my view there was perplexity to be disentangled, and confusion to be regulated.'

Johnson proposed to take a legal-style approach to fixing meaning. As the law often turns on precedents, so Johnson sought to find precedents of usage in language to establish 'the sovereignty of words'. Johnson was an avid collector of books and, as aids to his research for the dictionary, he gathered hundreds of volumes which he pored over for the precedents of usage that his method demanded – often scribbling notes and corrections all over the pages.

Johnson's friend, the author John Hawkins, wrote of his (Johnson's) working method: 'The books he used for this purpose were what he had in his own collection, a copious but a miserably ragged one, and all such as he could borrow; which latter, if ever they came back to those that lent them, were so defaced as to be scarce worth owning.'

After nine years of intense labour (Johnson had originally boasted to the publishers he could finish the project in three years), Johnson's dictionary was published on 15 April 1755. It contained 42,773 words with definitions and 'illustrations'. Johnson's 'illustrations' were in the form of literary quotations, highlighting usage in context, of which over 114,000 appear in the final text. Johnson employed a team of six clerks to transcribe the quotations into the completed draft; all other commentary, however, was composed by Johnson's own hand.

The dictionary met with great critical acclaim on publication, largely out of respect for the huge scale of the project. A similar endeavour undertaken in France by the Académie française had taken a team of forty scholars half a century to complete. However, the idiosyncratic and sometimes pompous style Johnson adopted in some of his commentary, also had its detractors.

Johnson deliberately omitted certain words that he personally thought did not warrant inclusion (words such as 'bang', 'grubby' and 'fuss'), while he included many obscure and archaic words such as 'Kickshaw':

KICKSHAW: A dish so changed by the cookery that it can scarcely be known.

Johnson often couldn't resist putting in his own personal, political and occasionally prejudiced views on the correct definition of certain words:

EXCISE: A hateful tax levied upon commodities, and adjudged not by the common judges of property, but wretches hired by those to whom excise is paid.
OATS: A grain, which in England is generally given to horses, but in Scotland appears to support the people.
MONSIEUR: A term of reproach for a Frenchman.
TORY: One who adheres to the ancient constitution of the state, and the apostolical hierarchy of the church of England, opposed to a Whig.
WHIG: The name of a faction. (Johnson was a staunch supporter of the Tory party.)

Although there is often sly wit at work in Johnson's definitions, there are also glaring errors too. There are also words which Johnson simply invented for his own amusement.

The main achievement of Johnson's dictionary is the copious use of literary quotations in his illustrations, a testament to the scale of his scholarship and learning. The following entry for the word 'zany' shows the depth of enquiry that Johnson undertook in compiling his dictionary which, despite its flaws, had a big influence on Noah Webster's dictionary in America, and was used as the starting point for the *Oxford English Dictionary*:

> ZA'NY. *n. s.* [probably of *zanei*. The contraction of Giovanni or sanna, a scoff, according to Skinner.] One employed to raise laughter by his gestures, actions and speeches; a merry Andrew; a buffoon.
> 'Some carrytale, some pleaseman, some slight zany,
> Some mumblenews, some trencher knight, some Dick,
> Told our intents before.' *Shakespeare.*

> 'Then write that I may follow, and so be
> Thy echo, thy debtor, thy foil, thy zany,
> I shall be thought, if mine like thine I shape,
> All the world's lion, though I be thy ape.' *Donne.*

> 'Oh, great restorer of the good old stage,
> Preacher at once, and zany of thy age.' *Pope's Dunciad.*

Did Samuel Johnson Have Tourette Syndrome?

Samuel Johnson was plagued by poor health throughout his life. He was so sick in early infancy that a priest was summoned several times to perform the last rites. In a parade of ailments, including tuberculosis, testicular cancer and bouts of chronic depression, one interesting posthumous diagnosis is that Johnson also had Tourette syndrome.

James Boswell and other biographers have provided descriptions of Johnson's seemingly uncontrollable tics, gesticulations and mannerisms, particularly when becoming animated or anxious. Boswell wrote:

> He commonly held his head on one side towards his right shoulder, and shook it in a tremulous manner, moving his body backwards and forwards, and rubbing his left knee in the same direction, with the palm of his hand. In the intervals of articulating he made various sounds with his mouth, sometimes as if ruminating, sometimes giving a half-whistle, sometimes making his tongue play backwards from the roof of his mouth, as if clucking like a hen, and sometimes ... pronouncing quickly under his breath, 'too, too, too'.
>
> JAMES BOSWELL, *THE LIFE OF SAMUEL JOHNSON* (1791)

———

The Hammer Blows of Grammar

Who climbs the grammar-tree, distinctly knows
Where noun, and verb, and participle grows.
JOHN DRYDEN, POET (1631–1700)

The huge increase in printed material during the sixteenth and seventeenth centuries contributed towards some standardization of English. However, it was obvious that more was needed. If Johnson's dictionary was to fix English spellings, then someone needed to tackle English grammar.

Grammar, the rules governing the language, remained very much in a state of flux. The history of English grammar is largely one of structures becoming simplified or dying out altogether, as opposed to becoming more complex or refined. The intricate verb inflections prominent in Old English and gendered nouns virtually disappeared by the mid-fourteenth century, and the Middle English period saw a cementing of the subject-verb-object word order and the Great Vowel Shift.

The English Renaissance and Restoration era saw huge advances in English, with thousands of words entering the language, but with this sudden growth came instability. Prominent figures such as Daniel Defoe and John Dryden suggested the founding of an Academy of English (along the lines of France's Académie française, established in 1635) to protect English from anomalies and confusions. This cause was taken up by Jonathan Swift in a 'A Proposal for Correcting, Improving, & Ascertaining the English Tongue'(1712), which he sent to Queen Anne's chief minister, the Earl of Oxford:

'My Lord; I do here in the Name of all the Learned and Polite Persons of the Nation, complain to your Lordship, as First Minister, that our Language is extremely imperfect; that its daily Improvements are by no means in proportion to its daily corruptions; and the Pretenders to polish and refine it, have chiefly multiplied Abuses and Absurdities; and, that in many Instances, it offends against every part of grammar.'

Ironically, Swift's proposal is riddled with grammatical abuses that would be considered poor English today (particularly his penchant for capitalizing certain words for emphasis). Swift's suggestion was not taken up and an Academy of English has never been created, but, following the publication of Johnson's dictionary, there was renewed interest in fixing the grammatical rules of the language.

Between 1750 and 1800, over two hundred grammar guides and text books were published, with grammarians divided into two clear camps. On one side were 'prescriptivists' (such as Robert Lowth and Lindley Murray) who favoured adherence to strict rules and forms, and on the other 'descriptivist' theorists, who believed that the rules of grammar should be flexible enough to reflect and thereby incorporate changes in common usage.

Robert Lowth (1710–87) was an Oxford scholar and prominent Anglican bishop best known for his work *A Short Introduction to English Grammar* (1762). Lowth set out to analyse and describe what he felt to be common errors in English and illustrated his arguments with examples of grammatical 'clangers' in the writings of notable authors such as Shakespeare, Milton and Pope. Among Lowth's many bugbears are classic shibboleths such as the use of 'who' or 'whom', double negatives and ending sentences with prepositions, as Shakespeare's Henry V does when he asks a foot soldier 'Who servest thou under?' According to Lowth, he should really be asking 'Under whom dost thou serve?'

Lowth was the first commentator to propose the rule that two negatives in a sentence cancel each other out or create a positive, as in 'Nor did they not perceive the evil plight in which they were.' Lowth's arguments were taken up by Lindley Murray in his book *English Grammar* (1794) which was widely used in American schools.

By the Victorian period the 'prescriptivist' view had become dominant with the study of traditional grammar an entrenched part of any school curriculum. Unfortunately, prescriptivism took the study of Latin grammar as its model and attempted to apply Latinate methods of classification and analysis to the study of English grammar, often in areas where using such frameworks were problematic and confusing. Victorian grammarians were extremely selective in the range of texts deemed to be worthy of analysis and study, and frowned upon common and informal language forms.

It is unsurprising then that the study of grammar in schools became a byword for the most tedious and soporific element of the curriculum.

Was Bishop Lowth 'a Fool'?

Bishop Robert Lowth was, by all accounts, a learned and virtuous man, an Oxford Professor of Poetry and a prominent clergyman who would have been Archbishop of Canterbury had failing health not forced him to refuse the appointment. However, it is as the 'grandfather' of traditional grammar that he is best remembered, and it is in this capacity that opponents of prescriptivism have chosen to attack and pillory his work.

In the 1830s, the writers Thomas De Quincey and William Hazlitt attacked Lowth and his contemporary, Lindley Murray, for starting a process of grammatical dogma akin to 'intellectual despotism'.

Two centuries later, questions, arguments and controversies over English grammar continue, particularly in the use of double negatives that are a common feature of African-American Vernacular English.

In 2003, the American academic Scott E. Kapel set up a website titled 'Bishop Lowth was a Fool', systematically attacking many of Lowth's ideas about correct usage and his method of applying quasi-Latin structures to English. Does the kindly Bishop really deserve to be so fervently denounced? The answer is probably not.

Lowth wrote his grammar book for his youngest son, Thomas, to teach him what he (Lowth) believed to be correct English. Lowth uses Thomas's name in several examples throughout the book ('I love Thomas, Thomas is loved by me') and never intended to print more than a handful of copies to give to family and friends. Lowth's printer, however, seeing there was a gap in the market, decided on an extensive print run. Bishop Lowth's background was in classical languages, so it is not surprising this would influence his views on how English grammar should be correctly structured. Ultimately, though, his main motivation was to help his son to speak and write in the manner he felt to be correct.

The Language of Industry

The Industrial Revolution in Britain during the eighteenth and nineteenth centuries ushered in an age of advancement in technology and science. As Britain moved towards an industrialized society, there became a need to find new ways to name and describe these developments. Samuel Johnson deliberately omitted what he called trade words that had started to come into English as industries developed: 'I could not visit caverns to learn the miner's language . . . nor visit the warehouses of merchants, and shops of artificers, to gain the names of wares, tools and operations, of which no mention is found in books,' writes Johnson in the preface notes to his dictionary.

However, by the early nineteenth century, many neologisms (new word coinages) had entered the English language through inventors, entrepreneurs and scientists writing books, pamphlets and scientific papers describing and exploring the industrial age. The development of the textiles industry, for example, gave rise to its own vocabulary, with words such as 'carding', 'spinning' 'doffing' and 'fulling' used to describe the different stages and processes of spinning cotton into cloth. New inventions appeared and the creation of new nouns, such as 'jenny', 'gin', 'water-frame' and 'mule'.

The products of the cotton mills also required a vocabulary, with words such as 'crinoline' and 'lingerie' entering into common usage. Some of these new words were adaptations of old Saxon terms, others were borrowed from other languages such as French, Latin and Greek. 'Lingerie', for example, is taken from the French word meaning 'things made of linen', which comes from the Old French word 'linge' which translates as 'washable'. Other products were named after notable people associated with them. A 'raglan' was a popular type of overcoat and is believed to have been named after Lord Raglan, a nineteenth-century army general and diplomat. Similarly, the mackintosh is named after Charles Mackintosh, the inventor of waterproof fabrics.

The age of steam power saw the language acquire words such as 'hydraulic' (from the Greek meaning 'water organ') and 'piston' (from French, meaning 'pestle' or 'to pound'). The catalogue of the Great Exhibition of 1851 contains dozens of neologisms that would not have existed in English a hundred years before, all relating to the giant machines and inventions on display; words such as 'centrifugal', 'cylindrical' and 'oscillating'.

Naturally, this growth of industrial language was mirrored by a leap in scientific language. The language of chemistry, biology, physics and medicine borrowed lots of words from the classical languages, using prefixes and suffixes for technical terms such as 'bio', 'tele', 'ology' and 'gram' – as in 'biology' and 'telegram'. Developments in medicine also required names for new ailments as they were diagnosed and treated, hence the appearance of words in medical journals such as 'diphtheria', 'cholera' and 'tuberculosis'.

During the nineteenth century, over half of the scientific papers, journals and books produced in the world were written in English. By creating a language of industry and science, English became the language of the industrial age the world over.

The Language Factory

While spelling and grammar rules were now available to help standardize the written word, the spoken word was keeping ahead with the times. Not only did industrialism bring new words, it brought new urban dialects. As rural workers went looking for work in towns, they took with them their regional accents. People from all over the British Isles resettled during this time, packing into the overcrowded towns. Thus a mix of accents, vocabulary and expressions went into the melting pot – the language production line was working overtime.

———

American English and Webster's *Dictionary*

In 1620, one hundred Puritans boarded the *Mayflower* to sail to the New World. These people, known as the Pilgrim Fathers, were seeking the chance of a new, more godly life, that they no longer believed was possible on English soil. They eventually landed at what they called New Plymouth and began to build shelters. Although by February 1621, half of the settlers had succumbed to the harsh winter conditions, many more Puritans made the journey across the Atlantic. The settlers managed to adapt to their new land and soon set up thriving colonies. English had now invaded America.

Other pioneering explorers of the sixteenth and seventeenth centuries opened up the New World and lucrative sugar and tobacco plantations were established in the West Indies.

Noah Webster's 'Blue-Backed Speller' and *An American Dictionary of the English Language* (1828)

Noah Webster (1758–1843) was a writer, educator and social reformer who is principally known for his creation of a series of language text books and dictionaries. Webster was a descendant of William Bradford, one of the founders of the Pilgrim Fathers' Plymouth colony.

Webster studied at Yale University during the American War of Independence and served in the Connecticut Militia against the British. At Yale he was taught by the distinguished academic and theologian Ezra Stiles, who was president of Yale at the time, and inspired his life-long interest in American nationalism. On graduating, Webster taught in elementary schools, before being admitted to the bar in 1781.

Webster soon became disillusioned with practising law, however, and returned to teaching, deciding that through educational reform the new federal nation state could grow and prosper. Webster set up several small schools and during his time as a teacher wrote a series of text books entitled *A Grammatical Institute of the English Language*. This three-part compendium (published between 1783 and 1785) consisted of text books on the rules of spelling, grammar and pronunciation. The first part of the compendium, *The American Spelling Book* (1790), was revised several times and became known, from the colour of its binding, as 'The Blue-Backed Speller'. The speller proved to be a phenomenal success and became the standard literacy text book in America for over a century, selling an estimated 60 million copies by 1890; it is still in print.

It was Webster's contention that the English language had become distorted by the British class system and that his project aimed to rescue 'our native tongue from the clamour of pedantry'. The people, he argued, could only truly achieve freedom and liberty by sharing a common standard of language. His republican sentiments had led to a strong dislike of the British ruling classes, and this informed his ideas about speech and pronunciation. The British upper classes spoke certain words by cutting short or omitting the final vowel sound, for example in 'celebratory', 'laboratory' or 'cemetery'. In American pronunciation the penultimate vowel sound is spoken and slightly elongated.

Webster's speller set about simplifying the rules of spelling by omitting aspects that Webster believed were unnecessary, confusing or simply foreign affectations. The most notable changes were omitting the letter 'u' in words such as 'color' and 'honor', replacing the 'c' with an 's' in 'defense', and dropping double consonants in words such as 'traveler' and 'wagon'.

In 1806, Webster started the major project of his life: to create the first dictionary of New World English. Twenty-two years later *An American Dictionary of the English Language* was published. Webster's dictionary contained over seventy thousand words, including several thousand that had not previously appeared in an English dictionary. Following on from his Speller, *Webster's Dictionary* continued his project to standardize 'American' spelling by logical means. Thus words such as 'centre' and 'theatre' were written with the 'r' and the 'e' reversed, in order to reflect the inflections of American pronunciation. Other words such as 'plough' and 'masque' became 'plow' and 'mask' respectively.

Some of Webster's innovations eventually became absorbed into British English, such as dropping the 'k' on words such as 'musick', 'magick' and 'logick'. Other differences between American English and British English persist to this day, such as the American 'paralyze' for British 'paralyse', 'catalog' for 'catalogue' or 'diarrhea' for 'diarrhoea' and 'fetus' for 'foetus', and so on.

The first edition of Webster's dictionary didn't sell very well and so he started working on a revised and expanded version. He died just before completing the second edition of his dictionary, which was published posthumously in 1851. Although Webster's dictionaries were not a commercial success, they were highly influential in standardizing American English spelling and pronunciation and for recording the emerging American vernacular.

The Ultimate Worde Horde: The Story of *The Oxford English Dictionary*

*T*he *Oxford English Dictionary*, or *OED* as it is affectionately known (the abbreviation being something of an irony given that brevity is not the *OED*'s central purpose), is the acknowledged authority on English vocabulary and word usage the world over. The second edition of the *OED*, published in 1989 in twenty volumes, contains full entries for 171,476 words in current use and around 50,000 words considered to be obsolete or archaic. The preface to the 1933 supplement to the first edition states:

> The aim of this Dictionary is to present in alphabetical series the words that have formed the English vocabulary from the time of the earliest records [c. AD 740] down to the present day, with all the relevant facts concerning their form, sense-history, pronunciation, and etymology. It embraces not only the standard language of literature and conversation, whether current at the moment, or obsolete, or archaic, but also the main technical vocabulary, and a large measure of dialectal usage and slang.

Rich in illustrative examples and etymology, the *OED* represents a towering achievement in sustained scholarship, an ongoing and infinite project, as new words continually enter the lexicon of the English language.

William Chester Minor (1834–1920)

Various notable scholars and literary figures have worked as clerks, volunteers or researchers on the OED throughout its 150-year history, such as J. R. R. Tolkien and Julian Barnes, but possibly the most notorious was the convicted murderer William Chester Minor. Minor had been a surgeon in the Union Army during the American Civil War having studied medicine at Yale University. Haunted by the horrors of the war, Minor suffered from severe dementia and paranoid hallucinations and was discharged from the army. After a period of incarceration in a lunatic asylum, Minor moved to England in 1871. On 17 February 1872, in London, Minor shot and killed a man during an attack of severe paranoia and was charged with murder. He escaped hanging on the grounds of insanity and was incarcerated in Broadmoor Hospital for the Criminally Insane. Minor was still in receipt of a US Army pension and so had access to funds to purchase books. When James Murray advertised for volunteers, Minor wrote to him offering his services and, unaware of his background, Murray accepted. A prodigious reader, Minor became one of Murray's most diligent and effective researchers, sending hundreds of judiciously chosen quotations and citations into the OED team. It was only after several years that Murray became aware of who his star contributor was and visited William Minor in Broadmoor to thank him personally for all of his hard work.

The current word count of the online edition contains information on 600,000 words, with more words, usages and definitions added in supplementary form every three months. The Oxford University Press funds the research, revision and development of the project with a colossal budget of £35 million, a figure that fully reflects the size and scope of their endeavours. However, the origins of the *OED* were far less lofty and far reaching.

The dictionary began life with no connection to Oxford University but was the brainchild of the Philological Society, a group of London intellectuals whose principal interests were to 'investigate and promote the study and knowledge of the structure, the affinities, and the history of languages'. Disillusioned with what they felt to be the inadequacies of available dictionaries, three of the leading members of the circle, Richard Chenevix Trench, Herbert Coleridge and Frederick Furnivall, formed an 'Unregistered Words Committee'. The committee's initial object was to produce a report investigating the errors, omissions and inadequacies in contemporary dictionaries; however, by the following year it began to dawn on the three men that what was required was the creation of a new dictionary. The society gave the project the working title of 'A New English Dictionary on Historical Principles', and a team of around eight hundred volunteer readers was assembled. The plan was for the dictionary to, as far as possible, show illustrative examples of words in context. To this end the volunteers were assigned books to search through and write out correct usage of specific words in the form of quotations on slips of paper. The work was slow and laborious and the management of the project was hampered by the death of Herbert Coleridge from tuberculosis and Trench's church commitments as the Dean of Westminster. By the 1870s, Frederick Furnivall recognized that the sheer magnitude of the work they had planned required significant assistance and after some heated negotiations lasting several years, an agreement was signed with Oxford University Press (OUP) to adopt and ultimately publish the dictionary. The noted Scottish philologist, James Murray, was installed as a salaried editor in 1879 and began work in a corrugated-iron shed in his back garden. Murray sent out calls for more volunteers and continued with the working strategy of recording words in quotation form to define usage. Initially it was envisaged that the project would take ten years to complete but within five years Murray and his editorial assistants had only reached as far as the word 'ant'. Murray was forced by the OUP to relocate to Oxford, taking his iron shed with him, and further editorial assistants were hired to assist with the work. The dictionary was initially published in instalments or fascicles, progressing alphabetically through the English language. The first fascicle was published in 1884 with subsequent volumes and supplements appearing at regular intervals up until the completion of the first edition in 1928, seventy years after the project began, and was finally reprinted in full in 1933 under the formal title of *The Oxford English Dictionary*. Sadly, James Murray did not live to see the project completed, having died in 1915; he is, however, immortalized as the first editor-in-chief of the behemoth of words that is the *OED*.

The Language of Empire

At its peak towards the end of the nineteenth century, the British Empire covered a quarter of the surface of the earth.

Britain's loss of the thirteen colonies of British America during the American War of Independence (1775–83) had forced a rethink on colonial expansion and Britain therefore turned its attention towards Asia and the south Pacific.

Captain James Cook claimed the eastern coast of Australia and the islands of New Zealand during the 1770s and these outposts, along with the acquisition of the Cape Colony in South Africa, laid the grounds for the British Empire's dominance during the nineteenth century.

In India, the East India Company (EIC), established in England by Royal Charter in 1600, had a long-established economic, military and political foothold by the early 1800s, largely financed by the trade in opium and tea (India being strategically positioned on the trade routes from the East, and trading in silk, spice, tea and opium).

Given that the EIC was seen as having more than a few loose cannons at its helm, the British Government nationalized the company, seizing its assets in the process. Britain eventually took full sovereign control of India in 1858.

In 1813, the Royal Charter was renewed by Parliament and one of the stipulations of the act was to provide funds for educating the Indian population. One hundred thousand rupees annually was set aside from the company coffers to fund Indian schools and the act also set provision for Christian missionaries and missionary schools to be created. However, many inside the East India Company resented the use of the organization's money to pay for the promotion of Indian education and literature in Sanskrit and Arabic.

When the charter was due for renewal in 1833, the Whig MP (and poet and historian) Thomas Babington (later Lord) Macaulay gave an impassioned speech which, in 1835, resulted in the English Education Act as a legislative Act of the Council of India. Macaulay's main agenda was to advance English as a way to civilize the population and to promote 'utilitarianism' or 'useful learning': 'I have conversed both here and at home with men distinguished by their proficiency in the Eastern tongues . . . I have never found one among them who could deny that a single shelf of a good European library was worth the whole native literature of India and Arabia.'

The English Education Act led to the funding of schools and educational establishments that taught an English curriculum with English as the language of instruction. As more and more of India's population became versed in the language, English became the language of the law and administration in the sub-continent.

The East India Company employed many native Indian clerks known as 'writers' to work in their offices overseeing their commercial activities, and numerous English-speaking Indians worked for the Crown, helping to govern their own territories. As a result many words entered the English lexicon from England's period of rule in India, among them 'pyjamas', 'bungalow', 'verandah', 'jungle', 'curry', 'shampoo' and 'khaki'.

It is interesting to note, however, that in Gandhi's political pamphlet 'Hind Swaraj' (1909), the blueprint for the Indian Nationalist Movement, he highlights the spread of English as the major stumbling block to Indian self-determination: 'To give millions a knowledge of English is to enslave them. The foundation that Macaulay laid for education has enslaved us . . . Is it not a sad commentary that we should have to speak of Home Rule in a foreign tongue?' Today, English is one of India's eighteen official languages.

PART SIX

—&—

POST-MODERN ENGLISH

—&—

*'Viewed freely, the English language is the
accretion and growth of every dialect, race, and
range of time, and is both the free and compacted
composition of all.'*
WALT WHITMAN, AMERICAN POET (1819–92)

————

This final section is titled Post-Modern English.
Strictly speaking, the Late Modern Period hasn't
yet passed, and although English in standard form
has remained largely fixed for the last two centuries,
it continues to move onwards. Subtle changes in
pronunciation increasingly have an influence on the
way English is spoken and taught. New dialects and
creoles are forming, taking a grip, finding a voice. The
English language continues to grow.

The digital age has brought extraordinary changes in
technology and to the way in which people communicate.
Will English survive fresh challenges and continue to
show the resilience and adaptability that have helped it
to become a pre-eminent global language?

————

Slang and Euphemisms

I've found that there are only two kinds that are any good: slang that has established itself in the language, and slang that you make up yourself. Everything else is apt to be passé before it gets into print.
RAYMOND CHANDLER, AMERICAN NOVELIST AND
SCREENWRITER (1888–1959)

The English language is extremely rich in slang words and euphemisms. *The Oxford Dictionary of English Grammar* (1994) describes slang as 'Words, phrases, and uses that are regarded as informal and are often restricted to special contexts or are peculiar to specific professions, classes etc'. Slang terms also vary from region to region and differ between English-speaking countries. Slang words for the toilet serve as a good example: 'khazi' (cockney English), 'dunny' (Australian English), 'john' (American English) and 'jacks' (Irish English).

Tracing the history or development of slang terms or the use of slang is problematic. As it is, informal language is closely linked to social groupings and regions, and bears comparisons with the vastly different dialects that spread across Britain in the Middle Ages. Slang terms are conspicuous in the works of Shakespeare and Chaucer (several of the characters in *The Canterbury Tales* are extremely 'potty-mouthed'). In the sixteenth century, Thomas Harman wrote *A Caveat or Warning for Common Cursitors, vulgarly called vagabonds* (1566), which is often cited as one of the first works of sociology in English. Harman recounts stories he has collected from speaking to 'vagabonds' and includes a description of 'Thieves' cant', a colourful argot supposedly created by gypsies to obscure their criminal activities in common conversation. Thieves' cant features heavily in a genre of Elizabethan publishing known as 'Rogue Literature', slim books and pamphlets that described street crimes and confidence tricks, supposedly to make the general public aware of the perils of associating with the 'rogue fraternity'. Examples of Thieves' cant include 'peppers', meaning eyes, and 'wapping' to describe the act of sexual intercourse.

The Cassell Dictionary of Slang (1998) describes slang as, 'A counter language, the language of the rebel, the outlaw, the despised and the marginal'.

Although there is some truth in this description if applied to street gang culture in modern urban cities and other counter-culture groups, slang is also a more generalized form of language.

Often slang terms are used to indicate delicate or taboo subjects and by the eighteenth century several slang dictionaries had been published. *A Classical Dictionary of the Vulgar Tongue* by Francis Grose was published in 1785 and proved to be very popular, running to several revised editions. To read Grose's 'dictionary' now is to unearth quaint and gloriously politically incorrect phrases such as 'blowsabella' for 'a dishevelled wench whose hair hangs about her face' and 'Frenchified' – 'to contract a venereal disease'. Grose's dictionary paved the way for several other, expanded and enlarged studies into English slang during the Victorian era.

The Victorians were curiously obsessed with slang, or the 'common tongue', despite bringing in harsh censorship laws such as the Obscenity Publications Act of 1857, which imposed severe restrictions on publishers and resulted in the banning of works by Thomas Hardy and later D. H. Lawrence.

Arguably the most well-known form of English slang is 'Cockney rhyming slang'. According to the 1859 *Dictionary of Modern Slang, Cant and Vulgar Words* by James Camden Hotten, rhyming slang developed through the patois of the East End of London street and market traders in the 1840s. There are various theories as to rhyming slang's evolution, from the traditional criminal fraternity codes to a fashion for the traders to draw attention to their goods by shouting out colourful and humorous rhymes to attract customers. Common examples that have survived from the nineteenth century include 'apples and pairs' (stairs), 'frog and toad' (road) and 'trouble and strife' (wife).

In the twentieth century, rhyming the names of significant people became fashionable, although this also dates from the Victorian era with terms such as 'Duke of York' (walk). Examples of modern rhyming slang (it is common practice to omit the second half of the rhyme in speech) include 'Britneys' (pop singer Britney Spears = beers) and Ayrton (motor-racing legend Ayrton Senna = 'tenner' = £10).

The English language is particularly adept at creating euphemisms, usually to describe taboo or offensive words or situations. Euphemisms occur through a process of circumlocution, literally 'talking around a subject'. Often they are employed in place of profanities or more traditionally, words which may be considered blasphemous. In Modern English, euphemisms tend to be most prevalent when discussing awkward or sensitive subjects such as sex, death or bodily functions, with classic examples being 'spending a penny' for visiting the toilet or 'has a bun in the oven' to describe an unspoken pregnancy. Some euphemisms spring up out of institutions and enter into common usage. For example, to describe a person as 'a loose canon' is an old eighteenth-century naval expression regularly used in everyday speech.

English slang and euphemisms are often full of wit and verbal invention and are constantly changing. One of the problems with slang dictionaries is that they are quite often out of date as soon as they have been printed as new terms and expressions have sprung up and replaced old or out-of-fashion ones. As Francis Grose noted in the preface to his 1785 *Dictionary*, slang words represent 'freedom of thought' and 'give a force and poignancy to the expressions of our common people'.

Close to the wind

BBC English versus Estuary English

The term 'received pronunciation' (RP) was first coined by grammarians in the mid-nineteenth century and is usually used to describe Standard English pronunciation. RP is also known as Oxford English or BBC English on account of the *Oxford English Dictionary* providing pronunciation guidelines based on RP and the British Broadcasting Corporation's initial policy of promoting RP in all of their radio and television transmissions.

RP is not an English dialect. It is an accent and linguistic register closely associated with southern England and a particular social class. The fact that RP has become associated with English speakers of a privileged background is on account of its sometimes being referred to informally as the Queen's (or King's) English. Ironically, the accent actually has its routes in the East Midlands dialect of Early Modern English that spread down into London during the fourteenth and fifteenth century at the time of the Great Vowel Shift.

The social stigma debates surrounding RP have long been problematic. Daniel Jones, a noted English phonetician, used RP in transcriptions of common English words in his *English Pronouncing Dictionary* (1917) and defined it as 'everyday speech in the families of southern English persons whose men-folk [had] been educated at the great public boarding-schools'. Originally, however, the teaching of RP in schools was intended to promote neutrality. A. Burrell, a writer of

Victorian teaching manuals, wrote in 1891 that, 'It is the business of educated people to speak so that no-one may be able to tell in what county their childhood was passed.'

Daniel Jones later modified his definition from 'public-school pronunciation' to 'received pronunciation', using the word 'received' in its original meaning of 'accepted' or 'correct'. This notion of one type of accent being more acceptable, or having a higher cachet, than others continued and continues to provoke debate.

The United States has the largest percentage of English speakers worldwide and yet Standard American English does not correspond to RP. American writers have often gently mocked RP, a notable example being F. Scott Fitzgerald in his novel *The Great Gatsby*, in which the eponymous hero's speech is peppered with exaggerated English-isms.

Since the 1960s, social commentators have criticized the concept of RP as being 'archaic' and 'anachronistic' and reflective of unwarranted privilege or power. It is estimated that only three per cent of the population of Great Britain speak with received pronunciation and yet RP continues to be the basis for pronunciation guides in virtually all English dictionaries. RP tends to be most keenly observed in state institutions such as Parliament, the law courts and the Church of England.

David Crystal and other linguistic commentators have noted that RP itself has changed, as evidenced by comparing BBC news reports from half a century ago, and the BBC has made a conscious effort to use a wider range of regional or ethnic minority accents in their broadcasts.

In 1993, *The Sunday Times* newspaper published a front-page article under the title: 'Yer Wot? "Estuary English" Sweeps Britain'. The article proposed that Estuary English, to some extent a watered-down London cockney accent, was now the most prevalent form of English pronunciation. The term 'Estuary' refers to the River Thames, which snakes through a large part of southern England, and its estuary areas (particularly East London, Essex and Kent). Estuary English (EE), although in principle a regional accent (albeit with a considerable geographical spread), has certain aspects which linguists have cited as evidence of widespread usage, particularly in the broadcast media.

One common aspect is 'glottalling' or using a glottal stop instead of a t-sound in certain positions, as in 'take it off' ('take e toff'). However, this is not the same as omitting the t-sound altogether, as 'plate' still sounds different from 'play'. The positions in which this happens are most typically at the end of a word or before another consonant sound. Other identified aspects of EE include substituting a 'ch' sound for the 'T' in words like Tuesday ('choose-day') and omitting the 'ly' in sentences such as 'you spoke too quick'. The dropping of 'h' before vowels, as in 'have it!' ('ave it') is often mistakenly thought to be an aspect of EE but is generally considered to be closer to the traditional cockney accent.

Various theories have been put forward for the rise of EE. The creation, after the Second World War, of new towns on the fringes of Greater London in Kent, Surrey and Essex led to a movement of Londoners to these areas, causing the cockney accent to spread and diffuse. An increase in social mobility is also cited, as is a growing sense that RP marked a person out as 'posh' and therefore out of touch with everyday life.

In 1995, Gillian Shephard, the Minister for Education, speaking at the Conservative Party Conference, called upon teachers to 'eradicate Estuary English' as it was 'slovenly, mumbling, bastardized cockney'. This led to considerable debate about the merits of EE versus the increasingly outmoded RP, and concerns about 'declining standards'. If there is a glaring irony in the class war over correct or the most prevalent form of Standard English pronunciation it is that RP is used as the basis for the teaching of English as a foreign language all across the world. Thus, skilled foreign nationals with an aptitude for language acquisition speak 'traditional' Standard English far better than the vast majority of native speakers of the United Kingdom.

Singlish and Spanglish

In the twenty-first century, English continues to influence other languages. Two key examples of this process can be found in the hybridized forms Singlish and Spanglish.

Singlish

Singapore was a key outpost of the British Empire and was under colonial rule for 146 years between 1819 and 1965. Originally set up as trading centre by Sir Stamford Raffles on behalf of the British East India Company, Singapore came under complete sovereign control in the early 1820s. The British established English-language schools and English became the language used for governance and administration of the lucrative Far East trade routes.

Naturally, the English language found its way to the local population and mingled with southern Chinese, Malay and Indian languages to create a creolized form of English. One possible reason for Singapore English developing its own distinct character, is that the teachers of English in state schools in the nineteenth and twentieth centuries tended to be from Eurasian backgrounds (e.g. Anglo-Indians or Anglo-Chinese).

When Singapore was granted independence, the newly elected government chose to make English the official language of the state, principally to maintain its status in world commerce.

Standard Singapore English (SSE) is based in the main on Standard English and follows the dictates of Received Pronunciation. However, outside the well-educated upper middle classes, SSE is not the most prevalent form of spoken English. Singapore Colloquial English, more commonly known as Singlish, is very much the language of the streets and has elements which diverge noticeably from the official tongue. Words and phrases from Malay, Bengali and Chinese have been absorbed into Singlish and shoe-horned into English-based sentences structures. For example, the Malay word 'kena' is used as an auxiliary to denote physical contact with a negative outcome: 'kena whacked' (you got beaten), 'kena burned' (you got burned). Singlish sentences often begin with the topic of the sentence, in a manner similar to Chinese and Japanese ('This country weather hot one' (The weather in this country is very hot), 'I go train wait you' (I will be waiting for you at the train station). Singlish constructions also, particularly in informal speech, omit past tenses, plurals and the verb 'to be': 'He so funny', 'Yesterday I go cinema', 'You read much book'.

There is a tendency when reading the sentences above to see them as just pidgin English, but Singlish has established grammatical forms and conventions embedded in its basic English structure. In a sense, the simplifications and omissions apparent in Singlish are similar to the processes that occurred between Old English and Middle English, where complicated verb inflections were condensed and gendered nouns excluded.

The cosmopolitan aspect of Singapore's population has led to the spread of four different languages, English, Malay, Tamil and Chinese, and the cross-fertilization between the separate tongues has fed into the Singlish word horde. The Singapore government, however, frowns upon the use of Singlish, and in 2000 started the Speak Good English Movement, a government funded initiative to encourage the use of Standard English. The movement has attracted criticism from social commentators, who maintain that Singlish is integral to the Singaporeans' identity and culture. In response to the criticism, Singapore's Minister for Education published an open letter in Singapore's principal newspaper the *Straits Times* in 2008, stating: 'While Singlish may be a fascinating academic topic for linguists to write papers about, Singapore has no interest in becoming a curious zoo specimen to be dissected and described by scholars.'

Spanglish

In contrast to Singlish, linguists dispute the status of Spanglish as a creole or pidgin form of English and Spanish. The main reason for this dispute is that Spanglish is not a uniform dialect but differs from region to region. 'Chicanos' (second-generation Mexican-Americans) living in the region of the Texas-Mexico border in the southern United States speak a hybrid English dialect that is not shared with similar communities in California or the Hispanic communities in New York or Florida.

Spanglish, in so far as it exists, is a totally informal language without any clear rules or structures. The two key elements are word-borrowing and code-switching. Word-borrowing occurs when English words are 'parachuted' into Spanish, usually with little regard for correct pronunciation. Code-switching is the practice of shifting between the two languages during a sentence, for example: 'Que is that?' ('What is that?') and 'Me voy de shopping para the mall' (I'm going shopping in the mall).

The Shape of Things to Come?

In 1933, H. G. Wells wrote a science-fiction novel titled *The Shape of Things to Come*. The book was Wells's attempt to write future history from 1933 up to the early decades of the twenty-second century. He made several accurate predictions, including the outbreak of the Second World War and the creation of nuclear submarines. Wells also predicted that English and Spanish would become the dominant world languages and would eventually merge to become interchangeable – in other words, Spanglish.

Despite the reticence of linguists to acknowledge Spanglish, the status of Spanish as one of the fastest growing languages in the world, with an estimated 350 million native speakers, means that hybridized dialects of English and Spanish will continue to develop and grow.

Digital English

By such innovations are languages enriched, when the words are adopted by the multitude, and naturalized by custom.

MIGUEL DE CERVANTES, SPANISH NOVELIST
(1547–1616)

In March 1975, a group of Californian electronics enthusiasts met up and formed the Homebrew Computer Club. The group comprised a loose collective of amateur computer scientists who were interested in developing new technology and building home computers. The club produced a newsletter and members exchanged ideas about programming and swapped electronic parts. The group proved to be highly influential in the creation of personal computers. Among their number were pivotal figures in computer technology such as Steve Jobs, co-founder of Apple Inc., and Bill Gates of Microsoft.

With the rapid advances in computer technology in the 1980s and 1990s, came a rapid expansion in computer terminology. The Homebrew Computer Club's newsletter was instrumental in disseminating the language of the digital age and much of the computer jargon that is common in the twenty-first century can be attributed to these early computer pioneers. Words such as 'microchip', 'hacker', 'server', 'memory card' and 'interface' all derive from this period, and as the use of computers became widespread, so the language used to describe the new technology entered the common lexicon.

By the mid 1990s, the Internet and the World Wide Web had become firmly established, and the extraordinary growth of websites, alongside developments in cell phones and other personal communication devices, has had a profound effect on English as a global language. It is estimated that 60 per cent of the content on web pages is composed in English and that nearly a third of Internet users worldwide have English as a first language.

One basic reason for English language dominance on the web is that most of the early computer-programming languages, protocols, codes and commands (such as ASCII) are based on the English alphabet. Computer scientists from non-English speaking countries would have needed to have some knowledge and grounding in English. ASCII (American Standard Code for Information Interchange) only supported 256 characters and so the more complex symbols of the Chinese, Cyrillic and Japanese alphabets could not be easily represented.

Modern computer-speak is littered with initialisms based on English, such as 'FTP' (File Transfer Protocol), 'DOS' (Disk Operating System) and 'ADPCM' (Adaptive Digital Pulse Code Modulation). The use of English abbreviations and mnemonics by programmers also fed into the language of computer users. New methods of communication such as email, chat rooms and text messaging quickly began to develop their own shorthand or meta-language. This new 'netspeak' involved various elements that have rapidly become established conventions of communication on the World Wide

Web. Alongside acronyms (LOL – 'laughing out loud'), common also are phonetic abbreviations such as 'C U L8R' ('see you later') and onomatopoeic spelling such as 'haha' to indicate laughter and amusement.

As the majority of online communication is regarded as informal, it has developed these conventions (particularly in real-time exchanges such as chat rooms or on social networking sites) as a way of mimicking face to face interactions. The informal aspect has also led to widespread eschewing of formal grammar and punctuation (particularly capital letters and apostrophes) in sentences.

Educationalists have voiced concerns about the effect that the Internet and new technology may be having on standards of literacy and, by extension, the future of the English language. According to the US Census, 60 per cent of American teenagers regularly send text messages or converse with their friends online, and this has been blamed in some quarters for what is seen as an erosion of their ability to use formal English. In one infamous incident, which received worldwide media attention, a teacher in Scotland received the standard, 'What I Did During My Summer Holidays' essay from a thirteen-year-old student written entirely in text speak: 'My smmr hols wr CWOT. B4, we used 2 go 2 NY 2C my bro, his GF & thr 3 :-@ kds FTF. ILNY, its gr8.'

However, other language experts argue that text or netspeak can benefit literacy. Digital English relies on speed of thought when encoding ideas into linguistic forms, and brevity and concision – which are valuable in writing skills. Furthermore, it is actually getting young adults to read and write regularly. Linguists such as David Crystal in his book *Language and the Internet* argue that far from altering or eroding the English language, new technology has expanded forms of communication and added thousands of new words and concepts to the lexicon. Crystal's principal point is that the Internet is still relatively new and that any substantial analysis of its effect on language needs to be monitored over an extensive period of time.

> We die. That may be the meaning of life. But we do language. That may be the measure of our lives.
> MAYA ANGELOU, AMERICAN WRITER AND POET (B. 1928)

SELECT BIBLIOGRAPHY

The following books provided invaluable resources of information in the research and writing of this book, and are recommended for further reading.

Ball, Martin J., *The Celtic Languages*, Routledge, 2002

Baugh, Alfred C. and Cable, Thomas, *A History of the English Language*,fifth edition, Routledge, 2005

Bragg, Melvyn, *The Adventure of English*, Sceptre, 2004
—, *The Book of Books: The Impact of the King James Bible 1611–2011*, Sceptre, 2011

Bryson, Bill, *Mother Tongue: The Story of the English Language*, Penguin, 2009

Burnley, David, *A Guide to Chaucer's Language*, Macmillan, 1983

Crystal, David, *The Cambridge Encyclopedia of the English Language*, Cambridge University Press, 2003
—, *The English Language: A Guided Tour of the Language*, Penguin, 2002
—, ed., *Samuel Johnson: A Dictionary of the English Language: An Anthology*, Penguin Classics, 2006
—, *Who Cares About English Usage?*, Penguin, 2000

Foster, Brian, *The Changing English Language*, Macmillan, 1968

Jespersen, Otto, *Growth and Structure of the English Language*, Doubleday, 1955

Merriam-Webster's Collegiate Dictionary, eleventh edition, Merriam-Webster, 2003

Onions, C. T., *The Oxford Dictionary of English Etymology*, Oxford University Press, 1966

Ousby, Ian, ed., *The Cambridge Guide to English Literature*, Cambridge University Press, 1996

Oxford English Dictionary, second edition (plus revisions), Oxford University Press, 1989, CD-ROM version 2009

Partridge, Eric, *The Penguin Dictionary of Historical Slang*, Penguin, 1978

Potter, Simeon, *Our Language*, Penguin, 1990

Pyles, Thomas, *Words and Ways of American English*, Random House, 2000

Winchester, Simon, *The Meaning of Everything: The Story of The Oxford English Dictionary*, Oxford Paperbacks, 2004

Wrenn, C. L., *A Study of Old English Literature*, Harrap, 1970

INDEX

P 158 laboratory, cemetery